truth: could it be true?

truth: could it be true?

peter hicks

solway

First Published 1996 by Solway

02 01 00 99 98 97 96 7 6 5 4 3 2 1

Solway is an imprint of Paternoster Publishing,
P.O. Box 300, Carlisle, Cumbria CA3 0QS U.K.

British Library Cataloguing in Publication Data

A catalogue record for this book
is available from the British Library.

ISBN 1–900507–16–1

Typeset by Photoprint, Torquay, Devon
Printed and bound in Great Britain by Mackays of Chatham PLC, Kent

Contents

Note on philosophical terms

Philosophical jargon and technical terms have largely been avoided in this book. However, a few have crept in and others have been included in the index for those wanting to look them up. Brief definitions can be found in the glossary following chapter 13.

I
Confusion

'When they had been running half an hour or so, and were quite dry again, the Dodo suddenly called out, "The race is over!" and they all crowded round it, panting, and asking "But who has won?"

'This question the Dodo could not answer without a great deal of thought, and it sat for a long time with one finger pressed upon its forehead (the position in which you usually see Shakespeare, in the pictures of him), while the rest waited in silence. At last the Dodo said, "Everybody has won, and all must have prizes." '

The Dodo's idea seems to have worked well for everybody except Alice, who had to supply the prizes. His approach remains very much in fashion well over a century after *Alice in Wonderland* was written. Lots of people are keen to apply concepts of equality and justice, and to reject the harsh 'winner takes all' spirit often found in our society, with its emphasis on competitiveness and success. Why should somebody be denied a prize simply because she is less clever than someone else, or able to run less fast, or less skilled in a specific area?

But has the Dodo got it completely right? 'All must have prizes' – yes, we may well be able to accept that, especially if we compromise a bit and have a first prize, a second prize, and so on to a ninety-ninth prize or whatever. But 'Everybody has won'? Does that really make sense? Perhaps it did in the Dodo's Caucus-race, where everyone ran where they liked when they liked. But will it work in the Football League, or the National Lottery, or in a General Election? In these areas it seems quite clear that not everyone can win every time. Whatever our ideas of equality and justice, if one team gains more points than any other, or if just one person gets the right numbers in the lottery, or someone tops the poll, we can hardly deny that they are in some way different from the others. They have come first; they have achieved something the others did not do. It is very hard to say they have not 'won.' In a parliamentary election the candidate who gets more votes than any of the other candidates has undeniably won; and if so, the others can't have won. However much we personally favoured another candidate, short of proving that the vote has been rigged, there seems to be nothing we can do other than accept the result. It is there. That candidate gained the most votes; our candidate got fewer. We may not like it, but those are the facts, and we have to accept them.

But suppose for a moment that we refuse to accept the facts; we go round telling everyone that Bristol Rovers and Nottingham Forest and Watford have all won the League; we storm into the Lottery offices and insist that everyone who bought a ticket should have the big prize; we commission an architect to redesign the Houses of Parliament so that every General Election candidate can take their seat. At first people might merely smile and think us odd. But if we persisted in doing this, they would soon tell us that this simply is not the kind of thing our society can allow people to do. If we are going to make sense of life and of society we have to fit in with the facts, the way things actually operate. We must not try to change the facts by forcing our views, however sincerely held, on to others. If we continue to go against the facts and start applying our 'everybody has won' principle to (let us say) driving at mini-roundabouts, or collecting the Chief

Executive's salary for ourselves, society will see this as a serious threat and start doing something about it. And if everyone started living by the same principle it would not be long before society disintegrated into chaos.

Rightly or wrongly, I personally have a lot of sympathy with the 'All must have prizes' approach. I would like to see the less intelligent or less able or less skilled being rewarded for their effort, whatever their achievement compared with others (though I have my doubts about everyone winning the Lottery!). But I cannot accept that 'All must have prizes' means that 'Everybody has won.' The two statements are saying different things, and it is simply muddled thinking to assume that 'All must have prizes' entails 'Everybody has won.'

Yet this muddled thinking lies at the heart of a huge range of ideas that are very influential in our society and often remain unquestioned.

John and Sally

John has been brought up accepting a standard Western scientific world view. For him matter is all that exists, and everything that happens is the result of scientific causes. If a tree falls, this is the result of the wind blowing, which is the result of a low pressure area, which is the result of conditions in the North Atlantic, and so on. It most certainly is not the work of gremlins, nor the hand of God, nor an answer to prayer. If things go bump in the night they must be material things making noisy contact with other material things for good scientific reasons.

One day John meets Sally, an anthropologist who has just spent four years living among a 'Stone-Age' tribe in Papua New Guinea, seeking to understand their culture. He is intrigued to find that Sally not only talks about the tribe's ideas and concepts, but seems to agree with them. 'Surely,' says John, 'you can't believe all that stuff about spirits controlling events and causing trees to fall and people to die and the like? After all, you came home by plane, and so clearly demonstrated your commitment to the Western scientific world view.'

'But I do believe it,' Sally replies. 'One of the main principles hammered into me while I was training is that in order to understand a culture you have got to be inside it. I've come to accept their way of seeing the world and what happens in the world – the dominance of the spiritual over the material, and the source of events being supernatural rather than natural – just as much as I ever accepted the scientific view you hold. In their system, it all fits into place. Why shouldn't it be right, for them? It's true that when I step outside their culture, I have to see things in a different way, like putting on a different pair of glasses. So coming back to Britain, and talking to you, I have to try and see things again in a scientific way. But who is to say that the Western way is any more right than theirs?'

'But they can't both be right,' replies John. 'You've been telling me about a man who died because the witch doctor put a curse on him. If a Western doctor had been there he would have found the real reason why he died; perhaps he was poisoned or something; there must have been a scientific explanation.'

'But he was examined by a doctor, and the doctor said he died of liver failure. But everyone knew that was because it was the liver that had been cursed.'

'But what caused the liver to fail? You say it was the curse, but I can't accept that. There must have been something wrong with his body chemistry or his diet or whatever. After all, if you started dying of liver failure I bet you'd jump on the first plane and get back to civilization and see a specialist pretty quick.'

'Maybe I would. But I don't see how that makes the Western world view any more "right" than the tribal one. The world of the spirits is a real one for them, and it is just as true for them as the scientific world is for you.'

'Perhaps so,' replies John. 'I don't question their sincerity or their right to hold their views. And if you choose to go and live among them, it may well work best for you to adopt their world view. But I still can't believe they are right. Either the world really is as they see it or it isn't. Either people die from curses or they don't. If my world view is right, theirs has got to be wrong.'

John's way of looking at the world may or may not be right; but he has a point. Granted, the tribal people have a right to their views; they have a culture in which their beliefs work quite satisfactorily. They are every bit as much entitled to a prize as 'Western civilization.' But do we have to accept that their beliefs and those of science are equally correct? Have they got it right? Do trees fall because spirits push them? Can a curse cause kidneys to pack up? Have they got the truth? Has John got the truth? And if one of them has got the truth, then surely the other has got something wrong? They cannot both have won.

Jenny and Michael

Jenny has just finished her first term at university reading for a history degree. She comes home to find her 11-year-old brother Michael struggling with a history assignment on the pattern of the English feudal system. 'Wow!' says Jenny, 'Are they still teaching you that stuff? Somebody should tell them it's all up for grabs now. No respectable historian accepts the traditional view. There are at least half a dozen new theories, all different, but all of them right in their own way.'

'But how can they be right?' asks Michael. 'If one theory says one thing, and another something different, how can they both be right?'

'Well, it's a matter of interpretation. There are all sorts of possible interpretations of the data, you know.'

'Maybe there are; but only one of them can be the correct interpretation, describing things as they really were. And if that one is right, the others must be wrong.'

'But we can never be certain whether we've got an interpretation right or wrong. So they are all equally right.'

'Rubbish; they can't be. Only one can be right. Suppose someone who was alive in those days got into a time machine and travelled forward to today. He'd soon tell all your experts what really happened and put them right.'

Would he? Could he? Are all the historians, with their differing views and interpretations, equally right? Undoubtedly, they are all equally deserving of a prize – probably the publication of a book outlining their radical ideas. But have they all got it right? Have they all won?

Alan and Tony

Alan and Tony find themselves working together for the Electricity Board, on a new installation. Alan is Conservative and Tony is Labour. Their conversation begins to warm up when they get on to the shortcomings of privatized railways.

'It's always the same,' says Tony. 'Once anything is privatized it goes down the chute. The only thing the private owners are interested in is profit; they don't care about ordinary people.'

'Of course they do. How are they going to get their profit unless people want to use the railways? The need to make a profit means a better service; it is the customer who benefits.'

'Well, I'd like to know when we are going to start benefiting. The Tories have privatized one thing after another and nothing has gone down in price or improved in service.'

'Maybe nothing has gone down in price, but certainly the prices haven't gone up as much as they would have done if things had still been nationalized.'

'Rubbish! Most prices trebled during the years of Tory government. If Labour had been in we'd have kept prices down.'

'How can you prove that? There's no way you can show that Labour would have done a better job than the Tories.'

'But of course they would have done – and for the very simple reason that Socialism is built on a firm foundation,

equality, the rights of the ordinary person, working together in a community, sharing what we've got, and all
that. Capitalism is based on selfishness and greed; anyone
can see it can't be right.'

'Hang on! Conservatism has got its principles just as
much as Socialism. It's just unfortunate that we've been in
power during a time of recession. If things had been easier
we'd have done a better job and been more popular.'

'But you can't prove that either. You claim your policies
are right, and when they don't work you blame something
else. Why haven't you the honesty to admit that you've got
the whole thing wrong from the beginning?'

Politicians – and their supporters – are pretty skilled at
holding to a position even when all the evidence seems to
go against it. Certainly they all deserve prizes for in-
genuity and effort. But, again, do we have to say that Alan
and Tony are both equally right? If Labour had ousted
Margaret Thatcher a year or two into her reign, would the
country be in a better or a worse state today? Some might
say that is a meaningless question, but it seems to me to
have plenty of meaning. Whatever has actually happened,
it must be true that either Conservative or Socialist
principles are best suited to producing positive results if
applied to the situation in Britain in the last part of the
twentieth century. If Conservatism is best, then Socialism
can't be best, and vice versa.

Lizzie and Sally

'There's no such thing as right and wrong, or good or
bad,' says Lizzie, throwing out the bait to anyone prepared

to bite. 'It's all relative. What's right in one situation will be wrong in another. What one culture sees as bad will be good somewhere else.'

'So it's right for me to have your drink,' tries Sally, reaching out for it.

'It might be, if you were dying of thirst; but you aren't, so put it down.'

11

'There you are; you do believe in right and wrong. Given our present circumstances, you agree it is wrong for me to steal your drink.'

'Ah, but that's only because you and I both belong to the same culture. In Britain it is against the law to steal drinks. If we were in Saudi Arabia it would be illegal to have a drink. And I'm sure it would be possible to imagine a society where stealing isn't wrong.'

'Yes,' says Sally, 'I can imagine it. It would be *awful*. In fact it would be unworkable; it wouldn't be a society at all – just anarchy. And that's the point: if we are going to live in society, we must have some principles, some fixed points, on which everything else is founded.'

'That may be so', replies Lizzie. 'But my point is that these principles aren't in themselves ultimate. They don't really exist. They are just a convenient fiction we use to keep people in order.'

'How do you know they don't exist? How can you prove that goodness and rightness aren't somehow foundational to the universe?'

'How can you prove that they are?'

'Well, I may not be able to prove it; but I can make a good case. I've already said that society can't exist without

basic principles of rightness and wrongness; and every-
where you look you can see what is right and wrong: it is
right for fish to be in the sea, and wrong for them to be
sitting up in trees; it is right for wildlife to be allowed to
live, and not exterminated by our greed. It is wrong to
make holes in the ozone layer, and so on.'

'But all you are saying is that you define goodness and
rightness in terms of the continuation of Planet Earth
roughly as it has been for the past few thousand years. But
how do you know that is a good thing? Maybe Planet
Earth is a blot on the cosmic landscape, and the best thing
would be to destroy the whole lot.'

'There you are; that's just typical. If you abandon good
and bad and right and wrong, you start by saying stealing's
OK, and end up destroying the earth. You may be able to
live with that, but I can't.'

I'm not sure who has come out on top in this debate;
certainly both Lizzie and Sally have a case. But we can
make the same point as before: if Sally is right, Lizzie can't
be right. If goodness and rightness are in some way
foundational to the universe, then it can't be true that all
moral issues are relative.

★　★　★

And then there was the man who decided that driving on
the left was merely a cultural convention, and worked his
way onto the wrong carriageway of the M1. His drive was
nasty, brutish and short. Full marks, I suppose, for trying.
But he didn't really win anything.

Mark and Jane

'Well, do *you* think I exist?' asks Mark, stretching himself
out on the chair.

'It looks like it,' says Jane, 'but looks can be deceptive.'

'That's what I'm worried about. Suppose it's all a
dream. Nothing is real. Nothing actually exists. There's no
point to anything.'

'But if nothing exists, you wouldn't exist, so you
wouldn't have to worry.'

'No, I suppose not. But I do worry.'

'Then you must exist. A non-existent thing can't
worry.'

'OK. Thanks. But how do I know that *you* exist? Maybe
I'm all on my own in the universe, and nothing else is
real.'

'In that case there is no point in carrying on this
conversation,' says Jane, getting up and walking away.

'Hey, no! Hang on. I was enjoying it.'

Jane comes back and sits down. 'That's one way of
telling that I'm real. I do things that are independent of
you and affect you. And what you say and do can affect me
in a real way.'

'But that can happen in dreams.'

'Not in the same way. When I dream I'm generally
aware that I am dreaming. But even if we're not aware,
when we look back, dreams are very different from real
life. In dreams you jump from one thing to another; things
happen that are impossible and illogical. In real life things
behave themselves sensibly; they fit together in a logical
and consistent way. Things don't chop and change like

they do in dreams. There's a kind of pattern, a givenness, a solidness, in real life.'

'But how do I know that I'm not imagining this givenness or solidness?'

'Just try walking through that wall over there.'

Here's another clear division. Both Mark and Jane have views that are quite tenable, but they are also quite incompatible. Mark is playing with scepticism; Jane has a strongly realistic view of things. If one is right, the other is wrong. They cannot both be right.

Stan and Rob

Stan is a senior laboratory technician. He is firmly wedded to the view of science he learnt as a lad: that scientists are 'discovering' things that are 'out there' in the universe. They work by forming a theory, a hypothesis; then they test it, and, if it is proved, it becomes fact: it is truth about things as they really are.

Rob finished his science degree last year. He has read Kuhn and Feyerabend and knows all about paradigms and epistemological anarchism. He cannot understand how Stan can think as he does.

'But science has never operated the way you say,' he argues. 'Theories only ever last for a limited time. All the things scientists believed last century have been rejected by scientists this century; and in twenty years all our current scientific text books will be out of date. Science today dare not claim to be discovering truth; all it does is produce short term working theories.'

'Is it a short-term working theory that water boils at 100°?'

'Well, it may be. But you can't deny that there have been radical changes in theories about the nuclear structure of hydrogen and oxygen atoms.'

'And you can't deny that water boiling at 100°, and the principle of gravitation, and thousands of other things have remained unchanged at the heart of scientific knowledge for centuries, and show no sign of ever being challenged. The problem with you guys is that you home in on some particularly obscure branch of scientific investigation, where there is still a lot of uncertainty, and make that the pattern for everything. I'll grant that sub-nuclear physics is still operating very much in the realm of theory; but most of science operates in the realm of established fact. It boils water, and puts people on the moon, and constructs computers. It operates in the real world, not the world of theory, and it works.'

'But sub-nuclear physics is foundational to everything. All your water molecules and spacecraft and computer molecules are made up of protons and neutrons and things. If the stuff that everything else is made of is unpredictable and indeterminate, that's got to affect everything.'

'And just how does it affect the boiling point of water? You show me some pure water that boils at 80° at sea level.'

A prize to Stan and a prize to Rob for some good arguing and sticking to their guns. But which one of them is right? Does science give us settled facts about the world as it is, or are there no such things? And if one is right, can the other be right as well?

★ ★ ★

A century or so ago practically everyone agreed with John and Michael and Sally and Jane and Stan. We live in a world that exists, that is real. We experience that world in all sorts of ways – through sight and touch, and living, and relating, and reacting, and so on. We don't always get everything right; we might have a mirage of an ice-cream van while we are in the desert, or see a distant tower and think it is square when it is round. But most of the time we get things right. And even when we get things wrong, we have ways of finding that out: we stagger towards the ice-cream van and it disappears; we get closer to the tower and can see its construction more clearly. Similarly with dreams; we may be deceived briefly by them. But we soon find out whether they are true or not by comparing them with real life. 'I dreamed I had been appointed Prime Minister, but nobody has asked me to move into Number Ten.'

So, according to this view, for most of the time we truly experience what is really there. And this shapes our knowledge. It may take time; we don't get to know everything at once. But we build up our knowledge in time. Other people, too, build up their knowledge. Very significantly, in almost all cases their knowledge tallies with ours and so helps confirm it. I measure the temperature of boiling water and find it is 100°; I try it again, and get the same result. Others try it, and they report the same. The result isn't something we put *into* the experiment. It is something that comes *out* of the experiment. We don't make it up. It is something outside of us; something given, something in the world; something we discover, and have to accept. We don't control it; in a way it controls us, causing us to think in a certain way and to hold certain beliefs. The more it gets confirmed, the more we are sure it is fact. Even if someone claims to have boiled water at 95° we don't easily abandon what has been so thoroughly tested. We check out the claim, and find, perhaps, that the person making it lives high up in a mountainous area. So we adapt our basic belief to: 'Water boils at 100° at sea level', whatever it may do on the top of a mountain or on the moon. In a sense the very challenging of the belief, and its ability to survive that challenge, makes its claim to be true all the stronger.

17

Such is what we might call the traditional way of thinking about our world and what we know about it. And I guess it is still the way that most people think most of the time.

But, as we have been seeing, it is one that has recently been challenged in all sorts of ways. The idea of fixed truth that originates in a real world outside of us, that we can discover, test, confirm, accept, and even submit to, is firmly rejected by some people. For them there is no fixed truth. Even if they concede that there may be fixed truth, they will point out that the fact is we can never discover it, or even establish whether or not it is there, so we have to forget about it and act as though it does not exist.

So all we have is a whole range of beliefs and ideas: different cultures and different individuals with different world views, different historical or sociological inter-pretations, different political principles, differing standards of right and wrong and good and bad, different theories about the nature of reality – lots of ideas and opinions, but no way of checking out which is the right one and which is wrong. One may appeal to us more than another; since we live in the world we have to adopt a set of beliefs, and most people more or less unthinkingly take on board the prevailing set in their culture at that time. But what we cannot do is claim that our set of beliefs is true, or that anybody else's is false.

Nor, of course, can a person who holds this position allow anyone else to claim that their set of beliefs is actually true. If truth cannot be known, then someone who claims to have discovered it must be wrong. There can be no final facts, no right way of seeing things, no universal moral principles, no specific winners. However much they may disagree, everyone is as right as everyone else. Everybody has won, and all must have prizes.

2
Doubt

I didn't like school. Some of the study I enjoyed. What school did for me I greatly appreciate. I was taught by some super teachers, and made many good friends. I even learned to enjoy the five-mile cycle ride each way, especially the downhill bits. But school as an institution isn't my scene.

I want to introduce you to three of my friends from school. I haven't had any contact with Mike and John since university days, and if either of them should get hold of this book and disagree with the picture I paint of them, I can only offer my very sincere apologies. My memory is doubtless imperfect, and I've a taken a bit of licence in representing the views of each of us in order to make the differences between us sharper. Doubtless, too, their views will have changed since those discussions at Bristol Grammar School in the 1950s; certainly the views I represent as mine have changed and developed quite a bit, and John came to the point of accepting the truth of Christianity round about the time he left school. I have kept in touch with David, who comes in and sorts me out at the end of the discussion, and he has continued through the years to show the wisdom and balance he contributes there.

Here we are, then, Mike, John and myself, sat in the form room of Upper Sixth Classical eating our sandwiches. Among the things we have in common is a disinclination to eat school dinners, and a lack of interest in rugby practice or secret smoking in the cellar with some of the prefects during the dinner break. Work at the moment is not too pressing; we've prepared our Greek for the afternoon session, and aren't interested in tonight's homework. So we pick up a topic we've worked on a number of times before: how can we know whether or not Christianity is true?

For me this is not a burning question. But it certainly is for Mike, who has been going to church for some time, but is struggling with doubts over what he has been taught. John's interest is much less personal. He is of an academic turn of mind and enjoys questioning things. He is at present very sceptical of the claims of Christianity, and I have a shrewd suspicion that even if someone was to provide him with a demonstration of their truth he still would be very slow to do anything about them.

David and John and Mike and Peter

Peter. How do you know your pickle sandwich isn't laced with arsenic? Your mother may have mistaken it for marge, or Sid may have put it in during break. And yet you're sitting there munching away happily. The fact is, you don't need to know. You are hungry; it is a pickle sandwich, and you eat it.

It is the same with Christianity. You don't need to know whether Christianity is true in order to ask God into your life. I asked him in, without stopping to ask lots of deep questions, and he came in.

John. You're right about the arsenic, but wrong about Christianity. I shouldn't eat the sandwich, in case it is poisoned. But, then, if I stop eating sandwiches, I will die, so I haven't gained anything. But I've lived happily without Christianity for 18 years, so I don't lose anything by not believing it now.

Peter. But you have to agree that whether it is true or

not, (and I'm sure it is), we've got very good reasons for taking it on board. Being a Christian is great; and what a fantastic place the world would be if everyone followed the teaching of Jesus. Even if there is a high risk of it being false, it is worth believing in it.

Mike. But that's terrible! It's a 'means justifies the end' 23 argument. I don't want to be a Christian because that will give me a great life, but because Christianity is the truth. Nor do I want a world (I think) that is a lovely place to live in but is founded on a lie. I'd rather have a tougher world founded on the truth.

John. But you're asking for too much, Mike. No one will ever be able to prove whether Christianity is true or not. We can never prove anything. You can't prove that that's a Mars bar you're about to eat.

Mike. Yes I can. It says 'Mars' on the wrapper; there you are.

John. But that doesn't prove it's a Mars bar. Someone may have taken the real Mars bar out and put something else in instead.

Mike. But it looks like a Mars bar . . .

John. A clever imitation.

Mike. And it tastes like a Mars bar.

John. Are you absolutely certain? Would you be prepared to swear in a court of law that this definitely is a Mars bar? Is it dead certain beyond all possible doubt?

Mike. No, I suppose not.

John. You can't be dead certain about anything. You'll never be certain about Christianity – either way, certain that it is true or certain that it is false. So you may as well give up, and just be sceptical, like me.

Peter. No, you don't have to be like him. You're eating that Mars bar because you believe what the wrapper says. You don't have to do a chemical analysis on the contents to make dead certain that the claim on the wrapper is true. You trust the label, just as John trusts his mum not to put arsenic in his sandwiches. It's all a matter of faith. Everything we do takes faith; we believe what people tell us, we trust the chair to hold up our weight. Faith is an essential part of life.

Mike. So you're saying that I've either got to be a sceptic like John or take everything by faith like you. I'm not sure that I want to do either. But, tell you what, each of you try and persuade me, to be a sceptic, or to take everything on trust. Whoever convinces me I'll follow. You start, Johannes Scepticus.

John. It's very straightforward. There is nothing in the real world that is not open to doubt. I can doubt whether that is, or was, a Mars bar. (Is it still a Mars bar, I wonder, now it is being transmogrified in your innards? When will it stop being a Mars bar, and become you?). I can doubt that you exist; I may be having a dream at this moment, a particularly nasty dream, and both of you are figments of it. Anything can be doubted, so nothing can be known. And if you can't know anything, you've got to be a sceptic.

It's useless saying 'Well, there's some evidence for it' or 'I'd like it to be true, so I'll assume it is'. That's like saying 'The earth is flat' because it seems that way to you and you don't like the thought of falling off the edge. Until you've absolutely finally proved it is flat (and you never could do that) you have no right to say or assume anything about it.

I rest my case.

Mike. Over to you, Petrus Fidelis.

Peter. Well, thanks, John, for making out such a good case for my side. There you are, saying you doubt whether Mike exists; you can't prove it; you're sceptical about that as you are about everything. And yet you sit there talking to him. You assume he's there; you can't prove it, but you take him on trust, just like I take God on trust.

We've just watched you eat a pickle sandwich here in this venerable academy of learning. If you really believed what you say, you would never be able to eat a pickle sandwich in case it contained arsenic. Nor would you come here to be educated, because you couldn't believe anything you are told. No one can be a real sceptic. They can only be sceptical about this or that, while continuing to believe everything else. Even when you started talking about the Mars bar in Mike's stomach you had to assume for that bit of the conversation that it really is a Mars bar. Scepticism doesn't work; you can't hold it consistently. The only thing the consistent sceptic can do is go and jump off Clifton Suspension Bridge.

So we all have to take things on trust. And why shouldn't we take big things on trust as well as little things? The existence of the USA as well as your mum's ability to tell the difference between arsenic and marge? Why shouldn't we take the biggest thing of all on trust – the existence of God and the truth of the Christian message?

You see, I'm not asking you to do anything different with Christianity from what you do with everything else.

Even John has to assume the existence of the world around him, and of other people, that his mother loves him and isn't out to poison him, and so on. The whole of life is built on assumptions and trust. We can't live any other way; even the biggest sceptic has to live that way. And, of course, it works. I assume that you exist and that I can talk to you, and when I start saying things you reply. I could be dreaming it all, but it doesn't seem very likely. In just the same way I assume God exists, and I commit my life to him, and it works. John would say I could be dreaming, or imagining it all, but I don't find that very likely.

Mike. Thanks. Well, I'll tell you my verdict: you're both pretty convincing. But I'm not sure that either of you is convincing enough. You're right, John; we can't get rid of doubts. That's the hell of it; I want to get rid of all these doubts; I hate them. But they won't go away. And Peter's right in saying that we all take things on trust; we couldn't live without it.

But I've still got problems. To go back to the Mars bar; there is a difference between being sceptical or trusting about that and being sceptical or trusting about Christianity. I've got no reason to be sceptical about Mars bars; I've always trusted that there will be a real Mars bar inside the wrapper, and there always has been. But I've got lots of reasons to doubt Christianity. There's all the stuff about the Bible that we get taught here. And at church they prayed for someone with cancer, and they died. And whatever Peter may say, when I've tried to live a Christian life I've found it pretty hard going.

So I can trust the Mars bar; but it takes a lot more faith

to trust the Bible. And I don't think it's primarily a matter of the size or importance of the issue. The USA is a big thing but I don't have any problem with believing in that. Eating a poisoned pickle sandwich could have pretty big results for whoever eats it (and for whoever put the arsenic in) but none of us really doubted that John's was OK. These are big things, but they're not a problem. Christianity is a big thing, and it is a problem because there seem to be lots of reasons to doubt it. But then again, I suppose there are lots of reasons to believe it too. I certainly accept that the Christian world view makes better sense of the universe, and if people followed it the world would be a better place to live in. And the case for the resurrection of Jesus sounds pretty convincing when you read *Who Moved the Stone?*[1] There's enough there to persuade me Christianity may be true; I can't just dismiss it out of hand. But what do I do with my doubts? Do I ignore them like Peter suggests, or let them have the final say like John says?

Peter. I don't think I'm saying you've got to ignore them totally. There are times when it's OK to face them, and work them through. I read *Who Moved the Stone?* partly because John had been producing all these arguments to show that Christianity isn't true, and I wanted to check out that there was good evidence for the resurrection. But life is too short to wait till you're certain about everything before you do anything. If you are down in the city centre

---

[1] When Frank Morison began writing *Who Moved the Stone?* he intended to disprove the gospel accounts of the resurrection of Jesus. But his research convinced him he had been mistaken and in the end he wrote a book arguing that the stories were true. First published by Faber in 1930, Morison's book is still (1996) in print.

waiting for a bus to get to school and one comes along marked Clifton, you don't just let it go because you're not absolutely certain that the driver has remembered to change the thing at the front, and the bus is in fact going to Temple Meads Station. You'd never get to school. You've got to trust what it says and get on.

John. 'Git on board, little children . . .'

Mike. But that's just the problem. Here I am, at Temple Meads, and there are two trains standing waiting. One is the train of faith; the other is the train of scepticism. How do I know which is the right one to get on board?

Peter. No! You still haven't got it. It isn't that one is the train of faith and the other is the train of something else. They are both trains of faith. John's world view is just as full of faith as mine. He assumes this, and trusts that. Atheists and agnostics and Marxists and pantheists and materialists and scientists and all the lot of them all start with faith; they assume certain things, and trust other things. Whatever train you get on, you have to exercise faith to get on it. Once you're on board, then it starts moving, and each train will end up in a different place. But faith is basic to getting anywhere.

John. No, I don't accept that. Faith is the very thing I'm trying to get rid of. You choose to live by faith, but I choose to take nothing on faith. You're wrong when you say I assume Mike or the Mars bar exists. I don't assume anything. I just may look as though I'm assuming it, for the sake of the argument; I've got to accept the usual conventions of conversation and look as though I think the person I'm talking to really is there. But I never actually assume anything. Mike's existence is still a totally open question.

Mike. Thanks.

Peter. So if you were really consistent, you would never be able to say anything? Or perhaps, if you are right, it wouldn't matter what you say in any case.

Mike. I'd like to ask Peter what he means by faith. He started off talking about trust and making assumptions, and then introduced the word faith. What is faith? Is it the same as trust and assuming something? I can accept that scientists have to trust their instruments and the like, and that they make certain assumptions about the consistency of the universe and so on. But I'm not sure that that's the same as faith in God. The preachers at my chapel talk of faith as a leap in the dark. If I mention my doubts they tell me to ignore them. 'Turn away from them,' they say, 'just have faith'. But what is faith?

(As Mike has been saying this, other people have been coming into the room. Dinner break is coming to an end. In a few minutes we've got to get down to Greek. David comes across and listens to Mike's question.)

Peter. Well, yes; the preachers are right. Jesus walked up to people and said, 'Follow me.' He didn't tell them anything about himself. He could have been anybody. So for the disciples it was a leap in the dark. He expected them to believe without any evidence. They had to decide there and then: 'What am I going to do with this man? Reject him, or follow him?'

Faith is a commitment. It is action. Faith isn't looking at a chair and saying 'I believe this and that about that chair.' Faith is sitting on the chair, and trusting it to take your weight. You don't know whether it will; someone may have sawn through three of the legs. But you commit yourself to it. That's the kind of faith God calls on us to exercise.

Mike. So he asks us to commit ourselves to him with no information at all as to who he is, whether he's good or evil, whether what he says is true or false, or anything?

David. No, I don't think he does. I don't believe the disciples had nothing to go on when Jesus called them to follow him. He'd been around for a bit. They'd heard things about him; maybe they'd listened to some of his teaching. No one would have been crazy enough to give up their livelihood and everything and follow blind someone they knew nothing about. And maybe there was something about him, a sense of goodness, the presence of God, if you like, that you could pick up even the first time you saw him. So they had something to go on before they took their step of faith.

But then the Bible tells us that not all the people who started following Jesus carried on. Some of them gave up and went back home. I don't think Christianity is a matter of a huge leap in the dark committing us to once and for ever faith. Some people tried it and found that for them it didn't work. The Bible says that this was because when they began to realize what some parts of his teaching really were, they didn't like it, and decided they'd had enough. But others, the more they went on with him, the more committed they became.

So I see faith more as a journey. You start off with a certain amount of evidence that there is a God, that the resurrection probably happened, that the Christian way of living and understanding the world is about the best on offer. So you decide it is worth trying out. You haven't got total proof of the truth of Christianity, but there's enough make a start on. Now Peter is right; you can in a sense only try it out from the inside. Christianity is not primarily a set of beliefs; it is a relationship with God, a way of living. So you've got to be a bit like the disciples; you commit yourself and start following Jesus. You begin the journey.

31

As you go along all sorts of things will happen. And they'll affect you in one of two ways. The disciples watched Jesus healing people, walking on the water, preaching and teaching, and the like, and for them it confirmed that first step that they'd taken. The more they went on with him, the more they were sure it had been right to follow him in the first place. I don't suppose this happened all at once. I guess there were issues that made them question and doubt, and maybe even Peter and Andrew and John were tempted at times to give up. But for the most part, despite the difficulties and doubts, the weight of evidence was on the side of Jesus, and they stuck with him. And that's what's happened to Peter here. I don't believe that, for all his talk about a leap in the dark, Peter would have continued believing in God if he hadn't had at least some confirmation that his belief was justified.

Of course, it is always possible that as you go along the journey of faith you find that instead of your faith being confirmed, it is being demolished. And then the honest thing to do is to stop following. The people in the New Testament who gave up following Jesus had found that his teaching was different from what they wanted. They thought the Messiah was going to be someone who would throw out the Romans by force. When Jesus made it clear he wasn't going to use force, they withdrew their commitment. We may think they made a mistake, but they were acting consistently with the evidence as they saw it.

So there's always a conditional element to faith. Paul says something like 'If the resurrection never happened, then your faith is empty, and you're wasting your time.' Suppose someone went to the tomb of Jesus in Jerusalem and found some bones and somehow proved that they were the bones of Jesus. However firmly we'd believed in the resurrection up to then, we'd have to say it didn't really happen. Now, Paul was quite sure the resurrection had happened, and so there is no risk of anyone finding any bones; and Peter may be justified in saying that nothing will in fact shake his belief in God. But if he starts saying that he is so committed to Christianity that he refuses to look at whatever new evidence anyone ever produces against it, he's on dangerous ground. He's got to admit that Christians do have reasons, however tentative, for putting their faith in God in the first place, and then further reasons for continuing to follow him. And it is always possible, however unlikely, that things will happen which make them realize those initial reasons were inadequate, and so they change their mind and stop following.

For me this is a much healthier way of looking at faith than the blind commitment for life way. And I think it is closer to the way science operates. The scientists look at the evidence, and on the basis of the evidence form a theory. Then they act on the theory. If it gets confirmed, well and good; if it doesn't, they abandon it.

Mike.   So you're saying that I don't need to get rid of all my doubts before I try out Christianity, as long as I feel there's enough evidence for it to have a test run. It's a sort of 'Lord, I believe; help my unbelief' situation.

David.   Yes, if you think there's enough to start on, start on it, and see where it gets you.

It doesn't get Mike very far, just at that moment, because it is time for Greek, and the intricacies of Sophocles' *Antigone*. But, doubtless, there will other dinner breaks.

33

3
Proof

Well over forty years ago, in a badly bomb-damaged school building, someone demonstrated to me and about thirty rather reluctant geometricians, that the sum of the internal angles of a triangle was always two right angles. I was fascinated. Any triangle? Every triangle? Big triangles? Little triangles? Squashed triangles? I even tried to design a triangle where the demonstration did not apply; maybe I could become famous as the discoverer of the Hix triangle, where the angles added up to 200°. But I couldn't. Nobody could. I had to admit defeat. The thing was impossible. The proof was total.

As I started writing this chapter, I tried to dig the proof out of my memory, where it has lain unused and unwanted for nearly half a century. To my surprise it came out readily enough, fresh, neat, and utterly convincing. The passing of the years hasn't changed it or dulled it. It worked as it has always worked, since my schooldays, since the days of the ancient Egyptians, and as it always will work, as long as there is anyone left to drag it out of their schoolday memories.

Now there's a proof for you. Memorable, neat, eternal, and utterly convincing. What an answer to doubt! What a way of convincing the sceptics! All they need is to go through the various steps of the argument, and they've got to agree to the conclusion. QED.

I can imagine that some might choose not to go through the various steps of the argument. They might insist that there is no way all the different shaped and sized triangles there have ever been could have angles that add up to 180°; there must be some that add up to 200°. Being sure of this they might refuse to listen to any argument, whether the geometrician's proof, or the views of expert mathematicians, or the experience of the ancient world, or the testimony of schoolboys.

So that neat and utterly convincing proof, whatever it has done for me, doesn't necessarily work for everyone. It is perfectly conceivable that there are thousands, even millions of people in the world who reject its conclusions.

★   ★   ★

The trial is over. The cases for the prosecution and the defence have been presented. The judge has summed up, and the jury have considered their verdict. The prisoner is guilty. The case against him has been proved. He can now justly be sentenced.

What was it that convinced the jury? Was it the discovery of the murder weapon in the boot of the defendant's car? Was it the evidence of the forensic scientist who showed that there were traces of the victim's blood on the defendant's clothing? Was it the fact that on the day after the murder he had deposited in his building society account the exact sum that had been stolen? Or was it the account of the neighbour who took his car number when she saw him leave the house and drive off just minutes after she had heard the victim shout?

Whatever it was, the jury were convinced. Something established the man's guilt. They approached the case, in theory at any rate, with minds completely open; now their minds are made up; they are sure. The case is proven.

But what sort of proof did the lawyer for the prosecution present? Was it total, undoubtable, such that anyone who went through the steps of her argument had to accept her conclusions? Certainly the defence lawyer didn't seem to find them very convincing. He had an answer for every one of them. At the time of the murder the defendant had been out looking for his car, which someone had 'borrowed'. He didn't find it till the next day, parked several streets away. On the front seat he found an old jacket with money in the pocket. Joyriders had 'borrowed' his car before, and damaged it; so he felt he had a right to pocket the money.

The prosecution had worked hard at salvaging her case. Why hadn't he reported the stolen car to the police? How was it the jacket was exactly his size, and the forensic scientist had found some of his hairs on the collar? How come he exactly fitted the neighbour's description? And so on.

Maybe it wasn't any one specific point that convinced the members of the jury. Perhaps none of the many aspects of the prosecution's case was sufficient in itself to count as proof. But add them together; and tie in the fact that the accused was one of the few people who knew that the victim had money in the house; and include the evidence that he was known to possess a knife identical to the one used; and take into account his confusion under cross examination . . . Added together, they made a strong enough case to convince; they totalled up to proof.

But what sort of proof? Clearly not the same sort of proof as the sum of the angles of a triangle. Yet enough to pronounce a man guilty, and have him put away for life. Enough to say 'We were sure.' Yet not enough, apparently, to convince the defence lawyer.

And what about those cases where juries pronounce

verdicts of guilty, but where many people are not convinced? They start lobbying; they dig up further evidence; they appeal; they take it to the Home Secretary. And eventually they win. The verdict is overturned. What was supposed to have been proved wasn't proved at all. What sort of proof is that?

Yet what would happen to our legal system if no case could be taken as proved until total clear cut angles-of-a-triangle proof had been produced and accepted by everybody? I fancy it would mean that no one would ever be pronounced guilty. That would mean the collapse of our legal system, and very probably the collapse of our society. It certainly would not mean that no one would ever be *guilty* of committing a crime. Lots of people, probably more people than ever, would in fact be guilty, but we would be unable to *prove* it.

We live in a society where crimes are committed, and people are in fact guilty. For all its faults, the British legal system as it stands seems to work pretty well; at any rate, it is hard to think of something acceptable that would work better. So we are generally happy to settle for a different sort of proof in a law court from that in a maths text book. The law court proof isn't anywhere near as neat; it isn't necessarily convincing to everybody (though even with the angles-of-a-triangle proof we saw that not everyone was necessarily convinced by it); and it may not last for ever – it could be overturned by fresh evidence. But it is still, for the purpose of a law court, a proof; and accepting it as such can have very far reaching effects.

★   ★   ★

'Edinburgh is further west than Cardiff.'

'Rubbish. Edinburgh is on the east side of Scotland, and Cardiff is right down in Wales. Cardiff is much further west.'

'No. You're wrong. Edinburgh is further west than Cardiff.'

'Prove it.'

'OK. Hand me that World Atlas. Here is the list of the latitudes and longitudes for all the towns and cities in the world. Here's Cardiff: 51°28' North and 3°11' West. And here's Edinburgh: 55°57' North and 3°12' West.'

'Wow! Who'd have thought it? OK. You're right. Edinburgh is further west than Cardiff.'

That was an easy proof: quick, straightforward, leading to full agreement. It worked so neatly because there was an established authority to which both sides in the argument could refer and which they both accepted.

I suppose it is just conceivable that the doubter might refuse to accept the authority of the atlas. She might insist on consulting other atlases or works of reference. But it is hard to imagine her continuing to be sceptical in the face of the unanimous verdict of every authority consulted.

So here is a useful kind of proof, founded on authority. It is something we use a lot, with a very high level of success. The authorities we call on aren't just books: 'I saw it on television'; 'She's knows all about the situation, so if she said it, it must be right'; 'I got it from the horse's mouth'; 'You can always trust Angela.' But they are such that we are ready to accept their verdict.

This is not to say that we are claiming some kind of infallibility for the authorities we use. The World Atlas prefaces its list of places with the warning that latitudes and longitudes 'in some cases are only approximate'. Out of nearly 40,000 listed some may be wrong. Even the maps themselves may not be drawn with perfect accuracy. But an atlas produced by a well-known publisher based in London is hardly likely to get Edinburgh and Cardiff wrong. The authority may not be infallible, but, for our current purposes, it is perfectly reliable. It gives us the proof we need.

* * *

Then there is another sort of proof: the 'seeing is believing' sort. We are not sure about something: that we'll get fewer colds if we eat more fruit; that you can see as far as Pembrokeshire from the top of Snowdon; that Roy has a great way of telling jokes. But we try it out for ourselves: we eat five pieces of fruit a day; we trek to the top of Snowdon (on a clear day); we have lunch with Roy. And, yes, we are cold-free; we can make out Mynydd Preseli; and we laugh our socks off. Our experience proves the truth of what we have been told.

In the scale of power to convince, personal experience must come pretty near the top. 'I've been there' – 'I've seen it with my own eyes' – 'I was there when it happened' – 'I've done it myself' – are all virtually unanswerable. 'However much you try and claim Bridlington is an inland town, you'll never change my mind. I've lived there for five years, and I know it's on the coast.' It is hard to think of a more convincing proof than that.

Of course, there are occasions when we misinterpret our experiences and so come to the wrong conclusion. We glance through the window on a dark night and see a ghost half way down the garden; we suffer from tinnitus, and think it is our neighbour using his drill. But experience has a built-in safeguard here. We look out of the window the next morning and realize that what we thought was a ghost was the white towel we'd left to dry on the line. We begin to have our doubts that it is our neighbour's drill when the noise goes on all night and when he's away on holiday. But, as a rule, such mistakes don't deter us from putting full confidence in our subsequent experience. The fact we've been deceived in some ways makes us even more confident when we have realized the mistake and found out the way things really are. 'I may have thought it was a ghost last night, but now I am sure it was the towel flapping in the wind.' 'When I found that the neighbour didn't even have a drill, I realized it was my tinnitus.'

So here is a pretty powerful form of proof. Since only a few people spend time with mathematical theorems or logical deductions, for most people this is the strongest form of proof available. It is certainly the most common.

* * *

Marie and Richard

Marie is 8. She is talking in the playground with Richard, who comes from a broken home and is very hurt and pretty worldly wise.

'How do you know your mummy and daddy love you?' asks Richard.

'Because they give me things'

'That doesn't prove they love you. My mum hates me and she still gives me things. It gives her a good feeling.'

'Well, they look after me.'

'That's only because they've got to. The neighbours would have the Social Services in if they didn't.'

'They say they love me.'

'Maybe they're telling lies.'

'But I'm happy when I'm with them, and they're happy when I am with them. My daddy plays with me, and laughs a lot when he is doing so. My mummy lets me do things with her and says how nice it is to have me helping her. They talk about me to their friends, and say how lucky they are to have a daughter.'

'But, don't you see? It's all put on. They are just pretending. They don't love you at all.'

What answer is there to Richard? Will he succeed in sowing doubts in Marie's mind? And if he does, how could Marie prove that her parents' love for her is real? How do you measure love?

The experience of relationships with other people, especially those close to us, is a key part of life, arguably at least as significant as keeping free of colds or seeing Mynydd Preseli. It is not an area where we would generally want to talk too much of 'proof'. Perhaps this is because in personal relationships we are more inclined to think in terms of things like trust and acceptance and love rather than the kind of mechanical demonstrations conjured up by the word proof.

But that is not to say that we cannot be sure or convinced in our personal relationships. Marie is (or was) convinced her parents love her. If Richard has managed to shake that conviction, and she runs home in tears, and cries, 'Daddy, do you love me?' then hopefully it will not be long before she is sure again. Equally, Marie's parents are sure that in her childlike way, she truly loves them. If you ask them, they may well say they are more sure of that than of any 'external' fact, like the location of Bridlington. They just know it; nothing can shake their conviction.

45

★ ★ ★

Logic is out of fashion. There was a time when no one's education was considered complete without a course in syllogisms and fallacies and undistributed middles. But, for all sorts of reasons, few people today see any value in the subject. Yet, strangely, many people still retain the concept of proof central to strict logic as the one and only form of proof they are willing to accept. Unless a thing is logically watertight, they claim, it cannot be considered proved.

The snag with this view is that nothing in the real world ever can be logically watertight. Take the most hackneyed logical argument:

All men are mortal.
Socrates is a man.
Therefore Socrates is mortal.

According to the logicians, this is a fine argument, and a total proof. But in fact it proves nothing. Suppose I were to claim that Socrates is immortal. Would the argument convince me? Not at all. The conclusion of the argument depends on the truth of its opening statement. And if I am convinced that Socrates is immortal I will reject the opening statement as false: it can't be true to say all men are mortal, since at least one is immortal.

What the argument is really saying is:

IF all men are mortal,
IF Socrates is a man,
THEN Socrates is mortal.

But that is saying no more than:

IF Graham is 50,
IF Sarah is 40,
THEN Graham is older than Sarah.

This is purely hypothetical; it tells you nothing about the real ages of Graham and Sarah, and so no reliable conclusion can be drawn. I happen to know that Sarah is 52, and has kept her age well in more senses than one. But all the logical arguments in the world cannot prove that.

★　★　★

We have not exhausted all the possible varieties of proof, but we have seen enough to show that there are many different sorts, each with different applications.

Out of this variety, we can perhaps formulate ten general conclusions on the nature and application of proof.

1. What will count as proof varies according to the sphere of operation. Proof in a court of law is different from proof in a geometry theorem. Being sure that someone loves you is a different kind of conviction from being sure that you actually exist.

2. We must not try and impose one form of proof (for example the logical or the mathematical) over the whole range of situations in which the concept of proof applies.

3. There is no proof that has the power to convince everyone. The defendant's girlfriend may insist on his innocence in the teeth of all the evidence. If someone wants to believe that you could have a triangle whose angles add up to 200° no one can force them to sit down and follow through the theorem that convinced me you cannot.

4. In some circumstances, for some people, a proof will be total and final. If someone doubts that they exist, the argument that they must exist in order to doubt may convince them once and for all. Whatever else they may doubt from now on, they cannot doubt that they exist.

5. In most cases, however convinced we may be that the matter has been proved, if pushed we would have to admit that there is a possibility, however remote, that we've got it wrong. Maybe for five years we have been deceived; we've actually been living at Scarborough, and Bridlington is midway between Bradford and Huddersfield. For all the weight of evidence, the case has been brilliantly rigged, and the defendant is innocent. Marie's parents are magnificent actors and in fact hate her.

6. Although we might have to accept this possibility of error, we still can be sufficiently convinced to take action, sometimes far-reaching action. The defendant is guilty and will be sent to prison for life. She loves

him and he loves her and they decide to get married. North Sea air is so bracing, and I buy a house in Bridlington. Indeed, if we wait for total logically watertight certainty before taking any action there is very little that we will ever do.

7. A good deal of proof is based on authority. Authority can be questioned, but life is too short to question every authority every time. So we take out a kind of season ticket. 'Yes, they are a reliable publisher; I've used their books several times and always found them right. I can accept what they say.'

8. For most people the strongest form of proof is personal experience. What we have seen or done ourselves is very convincing, especially if it continues to be confirmed by subsequent experience. Even the fact that we can on occasion make mistakes in our personal experience does not shake our faith in it. We know that on a dark night we may think that a towel is a ghost, but we have all sorts of ways of checking out and correcting our mistake.

9. Very often a proof is built up over a period of time from a number of elements. One piece of evidence in the law court may not convince us. But several pieces all pointing in the same direction, will. At the end of a 'Round Britain in a Week' coach tour we seem to remember Bridlington is on the coast. After checking with Uncle George (who lived in York for some time), and getting out a road atlas, we are pretty sure it is. When we have lived there for five years it is going to take a very great deal even to begin to shake our conviction.

10. One of the harder areas in which to prove something is that of personal relationships. Some may feel that any concept of proof is inappropriate here, because personal relationships are conducted on the level of feelings and trust and love and not of rational argument. Nevertheless, if Marie should ask 'How can I be sure mummy and daddy love me?' we could try and argue a case based on their words and actions and attitudes, and the fact that they are after all very bad at pretending.

4
God

Of all things people have set out to prove, the existence of God is the biggest. The stakes are high; the rewards are great. Those who believe in God, if they manage to produce such a proof, can justify their own beliefs, and, hopefully, win over unbelievers. Equally, of course, if they try and fail to prove God's existence, they weaken their case, and help confirm the unbelievers in their unbelief. And many an unbeliever has worked hard to turn the arguments on their heads and produce a proof that God does not exist, with the hope of thus undermining and destroying most if not all religion.

Speaking as a Christian, I am not entirely happy with the way that attempts to prove the existence of God have so often become the central issue for theologians and philosophers who wish to defend Christianity. After all, if we did manage to produce an argument that showed that God exists, we would still be a long way from showing the truth of Christianity. God could exist, and Christianity still be false. He or it could be the God of Islam, or the New Age people, quite different from the God of the New Testament.

So, for me, the task of proving the existence of God is not the key one. I am much more interested in seeking to prove the truth of the Christian package as a whole, that the Christian world view is the one that makes sense and works in the real world. But since a great deal of time and energy has been put into the task of proving the existence of God, we will spend some time looking at the issue.

* * *

Perhaps we need to recognize that the task is a slightly odd one in a couple of ways. Firstly, we don't, for the most part, go round seeking to prove the existence of things. We want to demonstrate whether the defendant is innocent or guilty, not whether or not he exists. We try and prove that Bridlington is on the coast, not that there is such a place. Secondly, there is, of course, something of an oddity in God himself. He doesn't fit readily into our usual categories. Some find it hard to form any idea at all of what God may be like. Some theologians have argued that God is so different from us he must exist in a totally different way, so that putting the word 'God' next to the word 'exists' is a waste of time.

However, I guess that most of us have something of an understanding of what the word 'God' means. We might have to paraphrase it in terms of 'the creative power that lies behind the universe', or 'a loving personal being as shown by Jesus Christ'. Similarly, though in general we take the existence of things as a given, we can cope with someone asking 'Do I exist?', 'Is the world real?' or 'Is there such a place as Bridlington?'. So, for the moment at any rate, that gives us enough to go on.

What sort of proof, then, are we after when we talk of proving that God exists? Is it a law-court type, or a logically watertight or a 'mummy loves me' one, or what? The answer to that depends to a large extent on what God is. If God is a postulate of geometry, then an angles-of-a-triangle type proof would be appropriate. If not, it wouldn't.

We've already mentioned a couple of answers to the question of what God is. Some would think in terms of the creative power that lies behind the universe. Others would think in more personal terms of the loving being revealed by Jesus. In the first case, God is a thing; in the second, a person.

If God is a thing, we might reasonably assume that the sort of proof appropriate to it is the proof we would apply to other things that exist. How do we show that there is such a place as Bridlington? How do we know that quarks exist? An answer here would be mainly in the spheres of authority and experience. Most people in the world have not had the privilege of going to Bridlington. Nevertheless, they accept the authority of the holiday brochures or the atlas or Uncle George. Even fewer people have experienced quarks. But the most recent books on sub-nuclear physics assure us they are there, and I've never met anybody who doesn't accept the authority of sub-nuclear physicists.

Behind the authority lies experience. Living in Bridlington for five years, walking along the prom, viewing it from a boat trip round Flamborough Head, all build up a case that effectively proves Bridlington exists. Quarks are a little more complex; no one has yet lived in one or seen one while on a boat trip. But the intriguing things that sub-nuclear physicists have experienced in their research can be explained effectively only by concluding that there are such things as quarks. To make sense of the basic structure of matter, quarks must exist.

Proof that we are experiencing God as an object is notoriously difficult to establish. We can't observe God as we observe Bridlington. Equally, we might add, we are on dangerous ground if we suggest that the inability to see

God as we might see the promenade at Bridlington is evidence that there is no such thing. Yuri Gagarin, the first Russian spaceman, announced that he didn't see God as he circled the world less than 200 miles above its surface; but that, I fancy, tells us more about Yuri Gagarin than about the existence or non-existence of God.

Quarks may help us here. No one has seen them, but we all believe they exist. They have to exist, in order to explain things that we (or some of us) experience. Their invisibility doesn't worry us, any more than the invisibility of the centre of the earth worries us. So it is perfectly reasonable to hold that in order to make sense of the things that we do observe, of the existence of the universe and of the various things we can see in it, we can legitimately conclude there must be a creative power lying behind it. God must exist.

If God is not so much a thing as a person, we might expect slightly different criteria to apply in answer to our question about the sort of proof that might be appropriate. Of course, we can treat a person as a thing. Perhaps, if we ask the question, 'Does Uncle George exist?' we are in fact treating him as a thing. We may be saying no more than, 'Is there such a thing as Uncle George's body?' If so it is the same sort of question as, 'Is there such a place as Bridlington?'. But when we are talking about personal beings, we want to talk about something more than just bodies. We are into the sphere of relationships. The issue for Marie is not whether her parents exist, but whether or not they love her. So if our concept of God is more along the lines of a loving personal being, the kind of proof appropriate when asking whether or not he exists is going to be the rather more nebulous type that is applicable in cases of personal relationships.

What is clear, whether God is a thing or a person, is that the logically watertight and the angles-of-a-triangle sorts of proof are inappropriate in proving whether or not it or he exists. We have seen that the logically watertight type of proof does nothing to establish the existence of anything. It is only ever of the form:

IF all men are mortal,
IF Socrates is a man,
THEN Socrates is mortal.

or

IF every house in Watford has a tree in its garden,
IF Hix's house is in Watford,
THEN there exists a tree in the garden of Hix's house.

This is an impeccable logically watertight argument, but you still have no idea whether or not there is a tree in my garden.

The same applies to the angles-of-a-triangle type of argument. Maths is a very satisfying subject largely because everything (or nearly everything) in it is so cut and dried. It is good to be able to say 'Two plus two equals four' and know that that will always will true; the answer can never be five. How simple life would be if all our knowing and thinking could be as clear-cut as that!

But we know that in the real world things are not as clear-cut as that. Very few things are straightforward. Complexity is the name of the game. A mathematician's triangle always has three perfectly straight sides and beauti-fully accurate angles. But in the real world no triangle is actually perfect. I have been doing some building, and have made myself a large 3/4/5 set square to make sure the angle of the walls of the rooms was 90°. I used the straightest pieces of two by one timber I could find. But though they looked straight to me they were still slightly out of true. I measured the sides as accurately as I could, and may have got within a fraction of a millimetre; but the set square is not precisely 3/4/5. Nor does it have a right angle of exactly 90°. No set square in the world has. But so what? I don't need the angle of the walls to be precisely 90°; somewhere between 89.9° and 90.1° will be quite acceptable, especially since I'm going to be doing the plastering.

Nor do I need definitive proof that the 348 bus is going to Carpenders Park station before I get on it. It is sufficient that all 348s are scheduled to go to the station, this one says it is a 348, I recognize the driver as one who has got me safely there many times before, and so on. In real life we have to work with slightly fuzzy edges.

So if the issue of the existence of God is an issue not of maths but something in the real world, then we should expect some fuzzy edges. The angles-of-a-triangle model, like the logically watertight one, is inappropriate.

★ ★ ★

Quite a few of the debates over the issue of proving the existence of God have made the mistake of adopting an inappropriate concept of proof. Unbelievers have demanded a logically watertight case. Believers have set themselves the task of producing a set of arguments such that anyone who worked through them would inevitably end up convinced that God really does exist.

We can understand this mistake to some extent when we look back at the historical setting in which the arguments for God's existence were put together. During the first sixteen Christian centuries theologians and apologists showed very little interest in philosophically proving God's existence. The arguments that were produced tended to be very brief, and presented within the context of faith, rather than as a means to try and convince unbelievers. The change came in the seventeenth and eighteenth centuries, a period when there was a tremendous stress on the role of reason. Reason was the judge of everything. If a thing could not be shown to be rationally provable it was unacceptable. For the early thinkers of that era, mathematics in particular provided a pattern for all arguing and knowing. Given the demand for this sort of rational justification of Christian beliefs, and sharing in the general thought patterns of their culture, Christians of the day set themselves to provide what was required of them.

So, for example, an argument that had been briefly mentioned some centuries earlier in the context of a meditation for Christians, was developed in the seventeenth century into a proof of the existence of God that, it was claimed, had all the force of a demonstration of a geometrical theorem. The argument claims that there is something in the very concept of God that makes his existence inevitable. If we think of God at all, we have to think of him existing. One way of putting it was:

> I have an idea of an infinite perfect being
> I am finite and imperfect.
> The nature of finiteness and imperfection make it inconceivable that I should be the source of the idea of an infinite perfect being.
> Therefore the source must be that infinite perfect being.
> Therefore an infinite perfect being exists.

Another was:

> God by definition is perfect.
> If a being has all perfections but lacks existence he is less than perfect.
> Therefore God exists.

Alternatively:

> God is by definition the greatest being conceivable.
> A being that exists is greater than one that does not exist.
> Therefore God exists.

Many people have felt that one or other of the forms of the argument carries at least some weight, and there are still philosophers today who put the argument forward as a valid one. But most find it singularly unconvincing. They may not be able to produce an answer to it, but it feels to them like a trick, a sleight of hand. Despite its logically watertight pattern, it doesn't convince.

* * *

For all the attractiveness of having a proof that can convince people of the existence of God in just a few lines of argument, we have seen that this kind of approach to proving the existence of God is not appropriate. More appropriate, since they tend to treat God as an object rather than a conclusion of a logical argument, are the proofs that start from the existence of things in the world and argue back to the existence of God.

These have taken all sorts of forms through the centuries. Here are some examples:

> Every event in the universe must have a cause.
> Each cause must in its turn have a cause.
> You cannot have an infinite chain of causes.
> Therefore there must be a first uncaused cause.
> This must be God.

A contemporary version of that might be:

> 15 billion years ago there was the Big Bang, which brought into being the causal chain of events which has resulted in the existence of everything in the universe today.
> Before the moment of the Big Bang none of the rules of physics, like cause and effect, operated.
> Therefore the explanation of the Big Bang must be sought outside of the world of physics, the natural world we are familiar with today.
> Therefore the supernatural must exist.
> Therefore God exists.

You could put it this way:

> Think of total nothingness, nothing at all existing.
> Nothing can happen, since there is nothing there to happen.
> Nor is there anything there to cause anything to happen, since nothing exists.
> Similarly, at no time can anything happen, and in no place can anything happen, since there is no time and no place.
> Yet the universe exists.

Therefore the existence of the universe cannot have been preceded by nothing.
Yet we know the universe had a beginning.
Therefore there must have been a beginner, something outside of the universe.
Therefore God exists.

Put this way, in the form we might use for a logically compelling proof, these arguments are open to criticism. But we might tone them down a bit, and say, for example: 'Of all the suggestions about where the universe came from in the first place, the idea that it was created by God makes the most sense.' This form of the argument might place us on safer ground. We are not claiming a logically watertight proof, but we are back with the towel on the line. There may be a number of ways of interpreting the white shape flapping in the darkness, but the one that makes best sense is the towel we brought back from swimming yesterday.

★ ★ ★

Another set of arguments focus on the way things are in the universe, rather than on the fact that the universe exists. But, in a similar way, they move back to the existence of God as the only or best explanation. So we get the familiar traditional argument:

If you were to find a watch while out walking in the country, you would justifiably conclude from looking at its complexity and evidence of design that it hadn't just come into existence by chance, but that it had been made by a watchmaker.

The universe as a whole shows much more complexity and evidence of design than a watch.

Therefore we may justifiably conclude that the universe was made by a universe maker.

Therefore God exists.

This argument, of course, carried a lot more weight in the days before the theory of evolution was generally accepted. Whole books have been written listing the evidences of design and purpose in the world, such as the human eye, the dandelion parachute, and the peculiar behaviour of water as it cools to near freezing (unexpectedly becoming less dense as it gets colder, so that the warmer water sinks to the bottom of the pond and enables fish to survive the winter), and arguing that these things demonstrate the existence of a designer, who is God. Most people today, however, would assume that evolutionary theory provides just as good an explanation of these things, if not a better one.

However, although this proof in its traditional form is very much out of favour at present, alternative forms of the argument have recently been cropping up, some of them coming from people with no religious axe to grind at all. A possible form would be:

The age of the universe is 15 billion years.

To evolve to its current state, and in particular, for life in the universe to evolve to where it is now, requires time, since it requires a long process of development involving a huge number of specific steps.

If that process and those steps occurred as a result of random chance, it would have taken a vast amount of time.

> It is inconceivable that it could have happened in the 15
> billion years available.
> Therefore the process is not the result of chance.
> Therefore something directed it.
> Therefore God exists.

Again, when we present this kind of argument in the above form, it may seem that we are claiming that it is logically watertight. But, recognizing that an argument for the existence of God should not be required to take the logically watertight form, we can adapt it and say something like this:

> It is generally accepted that in the comparatively short time
> available, the principle of random chance development is
> insufficient to explain how we have arrived at the very
> advanced and complex state we see around us.
> A number of explanations have been put forward, all of them
> involving some sort of concept of inbuilt direction, control,
> design, or purpose in the process.
> These concepts seem to be most readily explained if we
> postulate a personal designer or purposer who directs or
> controls the process.
> God would fill the bill.

This may not look like a proof in the logical sense, but in the towel-on-the-line sense it seems quite satisfactory. It is perfectly legitimate to look at the various ways of explaining how so much happened in such a limited time, and to decide that the existence of God provides the best explanation. The argument thus can be called a proof of God's existence, at any rate for those who are convinced by it.

★　★　★

It is fascinating to see how in the heady days of the seventeenth and eighteenth centuries, when reason was king and claimed the right to pronounce on the existence or otherwise of God, proofs put forward for his existence were rational and intellectual, seeking to argue in a logical way. Later, as reason's right to be the sole judge of what can and cannot be was increasingly challenged, other arguments, which were not so intellectual, began to be put forward. Perhaps unfortunately, theologians and philosophers were unable to cope with arguments that didn't look particularly logical; so they worked hard at dressing them up to make them look that way, or, if they didn't like them, criticized them as though they were meant to be logical proofs.

The first of these arguments was put forward by the philosopher Immanuel Kant towards the end of the eighteenth century and took as its starting point our moral sense of right and wrong, good and bad. Stated briefly, Kant claimed:

> We find in ourselves a moral principle which we know to be valid.
>
> We can explain the validity of this principle only if we assume the freedom of the will (so that we are able to choose to do what the moral law tells us we should do), immortality (so that injustice in this life can be put right), and the existence of God (to guarantee immortality, and implement justice).
>
> Therefore God must exist.

Kant stated clearly that he was not putting this forward as a logical proof of God's existence. Rather, God's existence is a necessary assumption if we are to make sense of the moral principles we find in ourselves and in society.

A more contemporary way of putting forward this proof for the existence of God might be:

> We cannot escape from the need to have moral principles by which society is regulated. Without them we will soon fall into anarchy.
>
> Individual moral principles need a foundational justification to validate them. For example, the principle that we should not kill other humans can be validated by the belief that the ultimate good is the preservation of the human race.
>
> A number of suggestions have been put forward as to what this ultimate basis for morality might be, such as the greatest happiness of the greatest number (of humans), the preservation of the environment, and so on. But for each of them it is possible to object that they do not provide us with something that is clearly the ultimate good. We can, for example, point out that the greatest happiness of the greatest number may not be a good if it is attained by plugging us all into pleasure machines, or if it is achieved by the ruining of planet Earth.
>
> The only candidate for a basis for morality that does seem clearly ultimate is God himself – a personal and wholly good God who has created us with the ability to make free choices and do good or evil.
>
> So the best way of providing a firm basis for morality is to accept the existence of God.

* * *

There can be little doubt that the type of argument Christians have used more than any other in defence of their belief in God, both in the many centuries before the coming of the Age of Reason in the seventeenth century, and even since, is the argument from personal experience. 'I believe God exists because I have experienced him. I know him. I talk to him in prayer. He's a personal friend of mine. We love each other.'

Again, those who either defend or attack this proof for God's existence, almost always tend to assume it must be of the logically watertight type. Since, as we have already seen, personal relationships do not fit very comfortably with strict logical demonstration, most philosophy books have tended either to ignore this proof completely, or dismiss it in a few lines. But there are few people who would not agree that personal relationships are profoundly important, for most of us considerably more important than the exact location of Bridlington. And we have already seen that though at their heart there seems to be something that is beyond the reach of argument, we can both question personal experiences in relationships, and think of supporting arguments that help demonstrate their reality.

We are back to Marie and her relationship with her parents. Richard has never known a secure loving relationship with his parents, and finds it impossible to imagine what it would be like. So he is very sceptical about Marie's claims, and doesn't find it at all difficult to cast doubt on them. Marie, for her part, finds it virtually impossible to convince Richard, though she herself is firmly convinced. Even if Richard should manage to dent this conviction, she knows what to do to restore it. As long as she is in fact experiencing her parents' love Richard is going to find it very difficult to make her change her mind. 'Whatever you may say, I just know they love me.'

For many believers, their personal experience of the presence or the power or the love of God is a perfectly valid proof of his existence. But, because personal relationships are personal, and, in particular, because God is a rather different person from our parents, it is notoriously difficult for one person, who has experienced God, to prove his existence to another person on the basis of that experience. Most likely the believer will not even try, but rather resort to something like: 'If you want to be convinced, you need to experience God as I have done. My experience will never make you a believer; it has got to be your experience'.

There is a lot of truth in this, but there is also a danger. It is a first step down the road that ends up by saying that my personal experience of God is so personal that no one who has not experienced it has any right to say anything about it. It thus opens up the possibility of people making all sorts of crazy claims about their experiences and then expecting immunity from criticism from others. 'I just know I've been getting messages from the Queen of Sheba. But I refuse to talk to you about it, because you've not had the experience.' I personally am not happy with this approach. I don't want Marie to run away from Richard every time she sees him in the playground. I tend to feel that, if Marie's parents really do love her, a relationship that goes through the process of being challenged and tested and thus becomes all the more firmly established is going to be a richer relationship as a result.

Equally, if Richard is right, Marie ought to know, however tough it may be. But more of this later.

* * *

Before we finish this chapter on proofs of the existence of
God, we will look at one further application of the
approach that claims 'The existence of God provides the
best explanation of the data'. This application starts from
human personhood, our consciousness, our ability to
comprehend the world around us, our freedom, our
creativity, our awareness of the transcendent, and the like.
Where do these things come from? Can we find an
adequate explanation for them?

Two types of answer are possible. One would say 'From
below', the other 'From above'. The 'from below' approach claims that the higher comes from the lower. Oaks
come from acorns; BMWs from Model T Fords. The basic
principle of evolution is that you start with something
simpler and out of it comes something more complex;
you start with the primitive, and from that comes the
advanced. So human personhood finds its full explanation
in spontaneous development from animals and early forms
of life and primeval soup.

The 'from above' answer points out that in fact acorns
come from oaks, and both Model T Fords and BMWs
come from the brain and creative skills of human beings.
Even the evolutionary process, like everything else in the
universe, came from the Big Bang, an event which is in
itself greater than all that has followed it; indeed, according to the second law of thermodynamics, everything
since the beginning has been in a state of decline and

degeneration. So the higher does not come from the lower. Everything comes from something higher than itself. If we are to find an adequate explanation for the existence of human personhood we must look not to primeval soup but to something that is higher than human personhood. It will need to be intelligent, since humans are intelligent, and if it was less intelligent than us it would not be higher. It will need to be creative, since humans are creative. It will need to be personal, since humans are personal, and so on. The best way of filling the bill is to accept the existence of God.

★ ★ ★

There they are, then: some of the many ways in which people have tried to prove the existence of God. Plenty have found one or another proof effective. Some have insisted that there can only be one sort of proof, the logically watertight sort, and so have failed to understand what most of the proofs are trying to say. But we have seen that not even the angles-of-a-triangle proof can force someone to accept its conclusions. Part of human person-hood is freedom; and part of freedom is the ability to say No, however logical or powerful the arguments may be.

5
Building

Not long ago I demolished a wall. It was an old wall, built with uncut natural stone. It was about half a metre thick and up to four metres high, and contained many tons of stone, mortar and rubble. It took me just an afternoon to demolish it totally using a crowbar and a heavy hammer. If I'd had a JCB or some other mechanical help I could have done it in half an hour.

I've also had a go at building walls in uncut natural stone. Its a slow process. The stones aren't designed for building. They tend to be round rather than square, and they come in all sizes and shapes. They don't fit readily together. You can only do one course at a time, or the weight of the stones above will squeeze the lower course out of place in the soft mortar. It has taken me weeks to build anything the size of the wall I got down in an afternoon.

But what job satisfaction! I had to fight the temptation to take a photograph every time I got a new stone in place, matching up its shape with those around it, checking its colour so that the overall effect of the many shades would look right, making sure that the mortar lines were pleasing to the eye. How satisfying to think that I had created something that looked good, and would stand for a hundred years or more. Maybe it made up for having to demolish that other old wall; the stones I'd saved I'd reused in my building; out of the demolition had come the new wall.

We all know that it is easier to break things than to build things, whether it is smashing crockery, writing off a car, or fouling up a relationship. We can all be negative and criticize and carry on about the government or the boss or whatever; it takes few brains and little effort to destroy. But it takes a lot more effort and wisdom to do something positive. However much we may shout our mouth off, few of us would be very keen to be in the Prime Minister's shoes, or would really make a better job of running the department or the company than the boss is doing.

And it is certainly easier to pick holes in other people's beliefs and world views than to build up and defend our own. Anyone can be sceptical; its a lot harder to get a vision and build up a set of beliefs, and to live by them and put them into action, to keep them going when things are tough, and defend them against those who choose to attack them.

This was graphically illustrated recently at a meeting I attended when a couple of speakers were asked to comment on the last fifty years in one specific sector of the Christian church. The first speaker attempted to analyze the experiences gone through and the lessons learned in order to extract some principles that might provide a basis for the next fifty years. The second speaker spent his time listing faults and failures of the past and showed no interest in what might be done to rectify them. His hard-hitting aggressive style gained him loud applause, but in fact he had contributed nothing to that particular movement. Those in it had already been told its shortcomings and mistakes many times over. What they wanted to know was where to go from there, and that was what the first speaker had bravely struggled to tell them.

Why is it easier to be critical than to be constructive, to be sceptical rather than to be committed to something we really believe, to doubt rather than to trust? We could think of various answers, some of them finding the reason in our basic psychology: some sort of Freudian aggression rooted in our need to assert ourselves over others, and pictured in the pleasure we used to get as children when we jumped on someone else's sand castle; or a Darwinian 'survival of the fittest' concept in which we ensure our survival by proving how unfit and stupid the other person is; or our basic perversity and failure to love, so that we find pleasure in damaging and destroying others; or our insecurity, which causes us to attack others first in case they attack us.

Doubtless there is a lot of truth in some of these suggestions. But, for our present purposes, we are going to focus on another answer, one that is practical rather than psychological: the simple fact that it is hard work to be constructive. Building is tough work; demolition is no-where near so tough. So we go for the easier option.

Suppose you had been appointed as research director of the Society for the Propagation of Goldfish, and your first task is to prove that all goldfish, though they may start out an uninteresting black colour, sooner or later turn gold, and are a credit to anyone's garden pond. You breed a few baby goldfish, and look after them well, and they turn gold. You try a few more, and the same happens. But a sceptical customer argues that those have turned gold because you've grown them in an indoor aquarium. So you grow some outdoors, and they turn gold. Then you hear of a couple of people, one in Penzance and one in John o'Groats, who claim to have elderly black goldfish. So you visit each of them, and manage to establish that their fish are in fact Siamese carp and not goldfish at all. You write an article, which is published all over the world in Fish Fanciers' Factsheet, and you get vanloads of letters in hundreds of different languages in reply. You work through each one, adding supportive evidence to your bulging files, and checking out apparent counter-examples. You give your life to the task; you grow old; you remain convinced of your case, but you never reach the point where you have conclusively proved it, however great the evidence you have amassed.

Meanwhile what does someone who wants to disprove the Society's thesis have to do? Produce one elderly black goldfish. That's all. Your case is demolished by one proven counter-example. It hardly seems fair; but that's the way it is. Of course, this may not be quite as easy as it sounds, especially if the Society's thesis is true; it may involve research, travelling, checking out Siamese carp, and the like. But, in theory at least, it can be done; just one elderly black goldfish disproves the thesis conclusively and finally.

And what does the sceptic have to do? Nothing at all. No travelling, no research, no experience needed. Simply the ability to doubt, to say, 'I don't believe the Society's thesis'. Undoubtedly the easiest option.

So, for an easy life, go for scepticism. For the hardest task, one that you'll never finally complete, go for a positive belief and work to establish it. For something in between, have a go at conclusively disproving other people's beliefs.

★ ★ ★

How then do we build up a belief or set of beliefs, whether we are scientists seeking an understanding of the world around us, or philosophers trying to establish what is real, or ordinary people trying to sort out whether or not God exists?

I suggest that we don't start with nothing. In fact I don't believe we can start with nothing, however hard some thinkers in the past may have tried to do so. We start with an idea, a theory, a hypothesis. We propose that water boils at 100° at sea level, that trees and tables and other people really do exist even when we are not looking at them, or that there is (or isn't) a God.

Secondly, I suggest that, in starting with the idea, we are biased. We don't select an idea at random, leaping out blindly and grabbing the first that comes our way. We select one we like, one that attracts us, the one we feel is most likely to be true. So, right from the start, we are not cold, objective, unbiased observers; there is an element of commitment in the way we approach the issue. Even if it is going to take hard work to establish our theory, we are willing to do it, because we believe in it, at any rate for the time being.

There's nothing wrong with this bias or commitment; we will be seeing later that such commitment is a basic part of what it means to function as a human person. It only becomes wrong if it is an unjustifiable commitment, if the counter-evidence piles up all around us and we still cling to our theory. But until that happens, commitment to our idea is perfectly justifiable.

Of course, our initial commitment may or may not have a good foundation. Our belief about colour changes in goldfish may be based on a few unusual cases where black goldfish had been fed exclusively on corn flakes. We may believe in God because we prayed for a bike for our eighth birthday and got one. That doesn't in itself make it false, although it does make it more likely that in the end we will find it is an unjustified belief.

Nor need our initial commitment be particularly large or strong. It can be fairly tentative. As we have said, it mustn't be so strong that nothing, not even masses of counter-examples, could shake it. But nor must it be so weak that we're not interested in it, or we'll never start the process in the first place.

Once we've started off with a belief, along with its attendant commitment, we can take the next steps, and begin to work out what we could call the implications and applications of that belief. Implications would be things like: 'If I sit on Brighton beach making a cup of tea the water I put on my Primus will boil at 100°' – 'The existence of physical objects in the world does not depend on me' – 'God could be the explanation for the origin of the universe'. Applications are more practical: 'I've over-filled the kettle and don't want it to boil over, so I'll take it off the Primus when the thermometer says 99°' – 'Even on a pitch dark night I'm going to walk round that tree, not through it' – 'I'm going to start praying, or developing whatever relationship I feel is appropriate between a human person and God.' We don't work out all the implications and applications at once, nor, generally, do we do it in a particularly structured fashion. Things occur to us; situations turn up; some beliefs we tuck away in the back of our mind and we do nothing about them for a long time; life is too short and too full to be philosophically analyzing everything all the time.

But as we do work out implications and applications, we react to them. We react in a whole range of ways, emotional as well as intellectual, personal as well as philosophical. Reactions will not be monochrome; some may be positive, and some may be negative. We like this implication, but aren't happy with that one. One application gets us excited; another raises problems. But, whether we actually think it out and verbalize it or not, we will tend to come to an overall reaction which will be either positive or negative, helping to confirm our initial idea, or making us feel uneasy about it. Such confirmation doesn't mean that we have reached the position where the thing is absolutely proved; nor do the things that make us uneasy cause us to scrap the idea right away. The process is long and often slow.

Then there is another important factor which comes into play as the process develops. Situations, implications or applications, come along which are open to more than one interpretation. The goldfish researcher is presented with a fish that could equally well be an elderly black goldfish, or a slightly unusually shaped Siamese carp. He will opt for the carp. The evidence, the shape, colour, age and so on of the fish, can be interpreted either way, and he interprets it in keeping with his basic belief and all the other evidence he has amassed along the way. But the good lady who has shown him the fish and believed for years that she has a black goldfish interprets the same evidence in a different way.

There is nothing wrong with this. It isn't that one is being honest and the other dishonest; both interpretations are possible, and both are doing right in interpreting the evidence within their own basic framework. In my experience, this kind of situation is pretty common. Somebody who is ill gets better; one person interprets it as an answer to prayer; another as a spontaneous remission of the disease. Both interpretations are valid; each person goes for the interpretation that fits his or her basic belief.

The variety of possible interpretations of some evidence, and the way we handle them and make them fit in with our basic concepts, explains why two people can hold incompatible sets of beliefs and continue to do so even though they talk together, examine the evidence together, and take all sorts of steps to find out who is right and who is wrong. It isn't that one is being perverse or stupid; given their position, it is quite legitimate to interpret those pieces of evidence that way.

But, of course, not all evidence is neutral. Some evidence, however hard we may try to interpret it according to our basic position, is awkward, embarrassing, and difficult to cope with. Here is a ten-year-old goldfish, spawned by parent goldfish of impeccable pedigree, reared and kept under observation by the most trustworthy of pisciculturists – and it is as black as your hat. Here is the president of the Flat Earth Society, getting off a plane that has just flown from London to Los Angeles to Auckland to Singapore to London. Here is an atheist who has just had a massive heart attack and finds himself standing before the great white throne.

Additionally, though we are quite justified in inter-preting neutral evidence according to our basic position, a large number of similar neutral pieces of evidence may begin to make us uneasy. We don't find it a problem to believe that just one or two fish breeders have got their tanks of baby goldfish and Siamese carp mixed up, and the carp have turned out to be shaped rather like goldfish. But when we are confronted with tens of thousands of the creatures, from all over the world, we begin to wonder.

What we do, if we are confronted with awkward evidence against our beliefs, depends both upon the strength of our beliefs and on the strength of the evidence. If we hold a belief very tentatively, perhaps because it is one we've recently adopted and still feel unsure about, it probably won't take much shaking. But if it is one we've held for a long time, and which we have tested lots of times and found very satisfactory, it is unlikely that we will let it go at once.

Perhaps three options are open to us. We may well start by trying to find some way of explaining away the counter-evidence, as in the case of the Siamese carp.

Alternatively, we may accept that we have no answer to the counter-evidence, but, equally, we have found that our set of beliefs has worked so well for so long, and been confirmed in so many ways, that we are reluctant to reject it on the strength of the counter evidence offered. The weight, for us, is still with the set of beliefs. So we keep the counter-evidence on hold and wait to see if any more comes along to reinforce it, or if something turns up that will explain it away. The person who is convinced that only physical things exist, and that everything can be explained scientifically, may, when confronted with good evidence for ESP and poltergeists and people dying as the result of the activities of witch doctors, concede that there is no immediate scientific answer to these things; but they are not sufficient to overthrow their materialistic world view. 'I accept that there is at present no scientific explanation of these things, but I'm sure one day we will find one.'

Thirdly, we may accept the counter evidence and take it on board. But instead of letting it destroy our beliefs, we choose to adapt them to accommodate it. Frequently, doing this is not too difficult. 'Water boils at 100°' can be adapted by adding 'pure' or 'at sea level'. 'The economy will prosper under the Tories' can be supplemented by 'unless there is a recession'. 'God answers prayer for healing' can be modified to 'We've all got to die some time, and although God heals some, he has to let some illnesses prove fatal.'

In any of these ways we can seek to retain our set of beliefs in the face of evidence that seems to count against them. There is no reason why we should not do this, and plenty of reason why we should. Given that the job of someone who wants to destroy a given set of beliefs is easier than that of the one who wants to defend them, it seems quite acceptable to show a certain amount of tenacity in holding on to our beliefs.

But there are two types of counter-evidence where we would be wrong to attempt the first or second of these three options. The first type is where there is a considerable number of well established counter-examples and their combined weight is clearly greater than the weight we attach to our beliefs. Here it would be wrong to try and justify following options one or two; we need to be honest, face the facts, and either go for option three, or abandon our beliefs. The second is where we have made a claim of the form: 'All black goldfish turn gold'. That kind of claim, as we have seen, can be conclusively refuted by one elderly black goldfish. If we make that kind of claim, we lay ourselves open to that kind of refutation; it is interesting to note that many of the claims of science are of this form ('All water boils at 100°') and option three is a very common reaction to conclusive counter-instances.

But the fact is that very many beliefs are not of this sort. We don't claim, 'Every tree I've ever thought I've seen really exists', or, 'Every time someone prays for healing God does a miracle.' Instead we temper our beliefs to agree with our experience: 'I believe that the vast majority of trees I think I see really exist, but I accept that on rare occasions I could be hallucinating.' 'God sometimes heals in answer to prayer.' These kinds of beliefs don't lay themselves open to the conclusive counter-example; the occasional imagined tree, and any number of people who are not healed, do not conclusively disprove the belief.

True, beliefs stated this way do not seem so neat and clear-cut. A statement such as 'All black goldfish turn gold' seems stronger and more like a textbook logical statement such as 'All men are mortal.' But I suggest the beliefs are none the worse for that. They are part of the real world, and, as we have seen, textbook logic is not part of that world. Even if he is right, the research director of the Society of the Propagation of Goldfish will never be able to prove conclusively in textbook fashion that all black goldfish turn gold. Neither the world around us nor the working of our own minds has to be simple and clear-cut all the time. It may or may not be the case that there is a fundamental logic to everything that exists and everything that happens; but undoubtedly the complexity of it all makes it extremely unlikely that reality can be reduced to a few simple logical formulae or proofs of geometry.

Two final points to notice in this section on building up sets of beliefs are that a belief that has gone through a time of testing will often emerge all the stronger as a result, and that beliefs tend to get more complex as they go on. Both these points are illustrated by the question of boiling water. Surviving the counter-examples, so far from weakening this belief, establishes it even more firmly. But it has grown from 'Water boils at 100°' to 'Pure water boils at 100° at sea level'.

★　★　★

Let's go back to Marie. She has a belief that her parents love her. Richard wants to demolish that belief. His task doesn't seem too hard. In their playground conversation he doesn't have to set out actually to prove anything; rather his approach is to cast doubts on Marie's parents' love for her by casting doubts on the evidence for that love. They give Marie things, they look after her, they say they love her − none of these, says Richard, proves anything. He is right; and the sceptic seems set to win hands down.

Marie's belief in her parents' love goes back a long way; it was there a good time before she became aware of it. She certainly didn't adopt it as the result of thinking carefully about the question, though her belief is none the worse for that. As long as she can remember, that belief has been there; she certainly could be said to be biased towards it or committed to it.

Even though she is only eight, she's already come across quite a few implications and applications of her belief. For her they have been positive, confirming and building up the belief, and developing her understanding of it. Her reactions to them have, of course, been much more than just intellectual. She has responded to love with love, and enjoyed other experiences like happiness and trust. These aren't things that can be neatly tied up in a logical formula, but, for her, they are very real, in a sense considerably more real than the bare statement 'Mummy and daddy love me'.

Richard appears to have limited his attack to casting doubt on the positive elements Marie was able to list as evidence for her parents' love. He could have gone a stage further, and proposed some counter-evidence: 'When you were in the shop the other day and you asked for an ice-cream, your mother said No'. Either way, Marie is quite right not to throw over her belief in her parents' love too readily. It is a well-founded belief, long lasting and frequently confirmed. It has worked well; she's happy with it. So she has good grounds for rejecting Richard's case, even if she can't answer it totally. She can deal with the ice-cream incident by explaining it away ('She didn't have enough money'), or by adapting her concept of love to incorporate it: 'Mummy says eating too much ice cream is bad for you; love isn't just giving people things; it is taking care of them and stopping them having things that are bad for them.'

We saw in chapter three that one of the main ways Marie faces Richard's scepticism is to go back to her parents and further experience their love. This isn't being anti-intellectual, but it is accepting that evidence for a belief does not have to be in the form of a pure rational argument; scepticism about whether trees really exist can be dealt with by trying to walk through one. For Marie the experience of love is a key part of her real world, far more real than Richard's clever arguments.

I suppose there is still a chance that Marie is mistaken about her parents' love. But for the moment she is perfectly justified in sticking to her belief and has good grounds for continuing to do so in the face of Richard's scepticism. Much more powerful counter-evidence will be required to justify her abandoning it. Indeed, it may well be that the end result of Richard's scepticism will be a strengthening and maturing of that belief.

★　★　★

One final point in our discussion on the way we build up our beliefs. We have seen that it is legitimate to be slow to reject a set of beliefs when faced with scepticism. Even counter-instances can be coped with in all sorts of positive ways. But we have also seen that sometimes it is right to accept a conclusive counter-instance, or the weight of a quantity of counter-evidence. Our beliefs are demolished.

But I suggest that even this is not a wholly negative thing. There are those who picture, say, the establishing of the Einsteinian view of the world as a total demolition of the Newtonian. Nothing could be further from the truth. The scientists who (mostly very reluctantly) accepted that Einstein was right and Newton was wrong in certain foundational principles didn't throw out everything they had learnt under the old scheme. Apples still fell from trees; water still boiled at 100°. Science didn't have to start again from scratch; much of the old package could be fitted into the new.

87

We are back to my wall building; my new wall was made up of stones from the old. We don't have to lose everything if we have to give up a belief. We don't have to go back and start from scratch. Others may do the demolishing; we can get on with building, even if building starts with salvaging.

6
Truth

Like many other things, truth has come in for a hammering in recent years. It isn't only that some of the things that we used to think were true we now don't believe to be true. The very concept of truth is under attack. We aren't just being told that this or that is not true; we are being told that there is no such thing as truth, at any rate in the generally accepted sense of the word.

A few generations ago almost everyone believed that there was such a thing as truth, and that there was more than a bit of it. In fact, there was a great deal of it, and it was growing all the time. Today the large majority of ordinary people still hold this view, despite the fact that those who are at the cutting edge of intellectual life have long abandoned it. In this 'traditional' view truth has certain characteristics which we can sum up under six points.

1. *Truth is outside of us.* It is not something that we create. Like the world itself, it is something we encounter; we are faced with it; it is there whether we like it or not, whether we look for it or not. Granted, it can also be inside us, in the sense that we can accept it and make it part of our thinking. But even if no one ever accepts it, it is still truth. When everyone thought the earth was flat, it was still true that it was spherical. Truth does not depend on us for its existence or its truthfulness.

2. *Truth is discoverable.* Somehow or other we have the capacity to discover truth. We ask questions; we investigate; we form theories; we test them; we seek evidence; we seek for further confirmation; we conclude that we have found the truth. The process may be

hard and long, with many false scents and setbacks. But, in this traditional view of truth, we are confident that despite the problems and reversals, we are steadily moving forward, learning, confirming, discovering more and more truth.

3. *Truth is authoritative.* We do not control truth. In a sense it controls us. Granted, we may manipulate it, or ignore it, or misrepresent it. But whatever we may try to do to it, truth itself is unchanged. We may misrepresent it, and tell a lie; but the truth remains. It provides a standard by which our misrepresentation can be judged. Though we may think it is to our short-term advantage to manipulate or distort it, we are always aware that 'truth will out'; when it is known, it will judge us, and if need be condemn us. Truth, then, is not something we manufacture or control or change to suit ourselves. Rather, the right attitude is to be open to it, accept it, and submit to it and its authority.

4. *Truth can be communicated.* Because truth is outside of us and able to be discovered and checked, we can learn truth from each other. We investigate different phenomena, we have different experiences, we see things from different angles; we communicate with each other, and thus help to build up a body of knowledge and understanding about the world. Of course, we don't always agree. One person says Edinburgh is further west than Cardiff, and another says it isn't. But truth is such that we are able to find ways, in our communicating, to settle disagreements. We can check the atlas, or consult the experts, or, if we refuse to

accept that kind of authority, we can set up some complicated experiment like timing sunrise in the two cities at the vernal equinox.

5. *Truth is the same the world over.* Wherever you are in the world, any specific truth remains the same. Whatever cultural differences there may be, and however much beliefs and ideas may vary, truth stays the same. Specific expressions of truth may appear to change; in France 'The law states that vehicles must be driven on the right' is true, while in Britain it is true that 'The law states that vehicles must be driven on the left.' But these truths are not contradictory. The seeming contradiction arises because the truth has been presented in abbreviated forms. All we need to do is unpack them a bit, to something like 'French law states that in France vehicles must be driven on the right' and so on, and the contradiction disappears.

6. *Truth is eternal.* Truths last for ever; they don't change after a time. Of course, specific applications of truth may only last for a time. 'It is raining' is true now, but, hopefully it won't be true this afternoon. But, again, if we unpack 'It is raining' a bit and say something like 'It is raining at 10.30 a.m. on January 21 1995 at Watford' we have a truth that will last for ever; nothing can change the fact of a miserable wet winter morning in January 1995. We could even claim that this truth stretches back in time as well as forward. It was true in 1066 that in Watford the morning of January 21 1995 would be wet.

★ ★ ★

This is the view of truth on which the development of modern science has been based and on which Western culture still depends. It has been tremendously fruitful; building on these six principles, a whole body of knowledge and way of seeing the world has developed and been applied to the business of living. Wherever it has been applied it has worked; truths we have discovered have been translated into machines and medicines and the many structures of our society.

Yet this view of truth has been consistently under attack for the last few generations, and has been abandoned by a large section of today's thinkers. For them, the six principles are to be rejected. Truth, as traditionally understood, simply does not exist. There is no *thing* outside of us, discoverable, authoritative, and fixed. If we are to use the word at all, we can think of truth only in terms of something that we each create for ourselves, something short-term, personal, 'truth-for-me'. What is true for me may well not be true for you; what is true today will not necessarily be true tomorrow. As Rob pointed out in his discussion with Stan, science has never 'discovered' anything; all it can ever do is put forward theories, short-term hypotheses which describe the way we see things at the moment, not the way things really are.

Why has the traditional concept been abandoned? All sorts of reasons are given, but I suggest they can be traced back to one basic issue, that of the justification of the traditional view of truth. How do we know that truth is as the traditional view says it is? Why is it outside of us, discoverable, authoritative, and so on? Granted, we do appear to be confronted with truth of this kind, and accepting it as such has been very fruitful, but how can we be sure that it is really there. How do we know we've got it right? What is the foundation, the guarantee of this truth?

Five approaches to truth 95

Through the centuries several answers have been given to these questions, all of which our contemporary avant-garde thinkers reject. We are going to look at four of them, and invite representatives briefly to state them and their reasons for holding them; we will also ask a contemporary thinker, Ms Sarah Post, to given reasons why she has rejected them.

Our first representative is Alexander Platonicus (Alex to his friends), who is speaking on behalf of a view which was first clearly stated by the ancient Greeks, and which has had supporters right up to the twentieth century.

Alex.   The matter is quite straightforward. When I see a tree I correctly conclude that there is actually a tree there, and that my experience of seeing branches and leaves and things is caused by the fact that the tree is there. What's more, the tree would have been there even if I had not happened to look in its direction. It was there before I saw it, and it will go on being there when I've stopped looking. It's the same with a truth. I come across a truth; I don't make it up; it comes to me and I 'see' it and accept it. But even if I don't accept it, it is still there.

Just where it is when I say, 'It is still there', I'm not ever so sure. It could be that all truths exists in some sort of place of their own, the realm of ideas. But more likely they exist in this world of ours, probably in the specific objects themselves. The fact of the tree is a basic part of the tree, like its trunk or its roots. When we see a tree, just as we are confronted with its shape, colours, beauty, and so on, we are aware of and accept its reality, the truth of its existence.

Sarah.   Alex, you are hardly going to expect me to accept a view that has been around for well over two thousand years. I would hope we've made at least a bit of progress since Plato. Even he had to admit that his concept of truths all sitting around in a sort of heavenly waiting room, ready for anyone who will come along and think them, is a bit far-fetched.

There are two big problems with your view. One is that we don't always get things right. Sometimes we are mistaken. We think we see a tree, and it turns out to be a mirage. So here is a tree that has shape and colour and beauty, but no reality or truth. If you can have one tree that doesn't include truth in itself, then all trees – all things – could be that way. You'll appreciate, incidentally, that I'm arguing here on your terms. I personally have major problems with the concepts of a tree's shape, colour, and especially its beauty, besides its truth.

The other problem with your view is that even you are going to have to admit that there is a radical difference between the physical properties of the tree and this thing you call its truth. Shape can be measured; colour can be analyzed according to the length of the light waves. But truth, how do you measure or scientifically analyze that? No one has ever managed to do it.

★ ★ ★

There are various things Alex could say in reply to Sarah, and plenty more she could say. But we'll go on to a second view, represented by Christianus Publicus. This was developed as Christian ideas met and engaged with the philosophy of ancient Greece.

Chris. You are asking for a foundation for truth, as we experience it. The answer is simple: truth is guaranteed by God. God lies behind everything; he is the creator and upholder not just of all material things, but of all other things as well. Love and beauty and joy all have their foundations in him. And so does truth. He knows all things; he knew them before the foundation of the world. The Divine Wisdom eternally embraces and upholds every truth.

If humanity had remained in perfect fellowship with God, we would share this direct awareness of what is true, since we are made in his image. But the human race is fallen. And, just as we do things wrong, we get things wrong. As Sarah says, we make mistakes. But not all the time; God has not left us without a witness. Our reason, that God-given faculty made in the image of the Divine Wisdom, though tainted, is not destroyed. Additionally, God has given us revelation in the Scriptures. Between the two, we can find enough of the truth to live and do the will of God.

Sarah. Sorry, Chris; it won't work. You know full well what you are doing. It is like young Johnny who tells a lie; when he's about to be found out, he starts telling another lie, to cover the first. You've invented these bogus things called 'truths' as basic to your view of the world. Now these are being challenged, you invent another bogus entity to bolster them up. And how are you going to bolster up God? By inventing something else? No, let's go for the simple life, and accept that there is no God and there are no truths.

★ ★ ★

For a third view we move forward to the seventeenth and eighteenth centuries, to the period when reason came to the front of the stage. Not that it hadn't always been important in people's thinking; but its significance had tended to be balanced by things like revelation and tradition. What happened in the Age of Reason was that everything else (and revelation in particular) was systematically rejected; reason alone was king, and judge of everything. Tom Brain will represent this view.

Tom. Sarah, you are absolutely right. Alex and Chris have cluttered up the world with all sorts of unnecessary objects. We need to clear the place out, so that the fresh clean winds of revolution can blow through. At last humanity has come of age; we can shake off the shackles of past beliefs, and be truly free. Reason shall be our guide. Whatever we can prove rationally is true; whatever cannot be proved, however attractive or long-cherished it may be, has to go. Let us follow the lead of the sciences; see how they are investigating and challenging and questioning and proving everything, building up a whole new view of the world. We will follow them, as they follow reason.

What, then, does reason teach us? First, that there are things we can be absolutely sure of. The internal angles of a triangle add up to two right angles. Any rational person can see that that has to be true. 'I exist'; I cannot rationally reject that. Here then are some undoubtable truths. Now, we don't have to start trying to find a place for these truths to exist, or drag in God to guarantee their validity. They are truths of reason; that is enough. What's more, just as the scientists are able to make deductions from the things they have observed, so we are able to deduce further truths from these basic foundational truths of reason.

So we have a clear way of telling what is true and what is not. Foundational truths of reason and further truths that can be rationally deduced from them are true. Everything else is false.

Sarah. But, Tom, all you have done is to substitute one authority for another. In the past, people have accepted the authority of tradition, or of God, or of the Bible. You reject these, and then ask us to accept the authority of reason. Why should we? Why should we accept any authority? If those winds of freedom you are so keen on are really going to blow, let's be totally free, and accept no authority at all.

And, in any case, you know full well that it is desperately hard to build up a body of rationally proved truth in the way you have said. Apart from truths of maths and 'I exist', no one has been able to find any foundational truths of reason that most people will accept, and some have even questioned those two. So all this talk about 'a clear way of telling what is true' is rubbish. It simply doesn't work.

★ ★ ★

Our final viewpoint is the most recent of the four, being confined more or less to the twentieth century. Mary Praxis will present it for us.

Mary. Sarah has pointed out that all the authorities we have called on in our attempts to justify the concept of truth have failed. If that is so, let's accept it, and stop asking for something that will give us certainty, and get on with the business of living. With all due respect to the philosophers, living is far more important than explaining everything. The philosopher may not be able to prove that her chair is there, but she still sits on it.

I accept that we need to have some sort of concept of truth; it seems to be essential for communication and knowledge. But we don't need to demand that anything guarantees or proves this or that piece of truth. Let's stop asking questions about whether what we think is true really is true. Let's get on with living. If we can live with something, if it works, if it is fruitful in discovering things and doing things, let's take it as a kind of working truth. If after a time we find it doesn't work any more, or something else looks as though it will work better, we'll abandon it, and go for the next thing.

Sarah. Clearly you and I agree for the most part. We both want to abandon fixed unchanging truth, and go for something far more fluid. But there's still a difference between us. Even though you've got rid of reason and God and the like as your basis for truth, you've still tried to introduce something else, another authority. For you the criterion is 'Does it work?'; if it does, then it is true, even if you allow that it is only true for the time being. I'm not sure I'm happy with this. It raises all sorts of questions about what we mean by 'it works'. How do I know it works? What if it works for you but not for me? Are you claiming that your pragmatic approach to the world is the right one, that it is true? If so, you are still hanging on to traces of the old view of truth you claim to have rejected.

★ ★ ★

We'd better give the final word to Sarah. If she rejects all the other views of truth, what does she put in their place? And what is her justification for that?

Sarah. That is just the point. I don't have a 'view of truth' to replace the others, if by that you mean a concept of truth we can all agree is the right one. I do accept that in order to get on with the job of living in the world I have to act as though some concept of truth is right, and Mary's pragmatic concept is as good as any.

But I refuse to allow that this means that anything we might be tempted to call true exists in any shape or form, other than in my own brain. Truth doesn't come to me from outside. I make truth. I create it, truth-for-me. You create your truth, truth-for-you. Nothing controls you or me as we create our truths; and the truths we create may well be totally different. It's like beauty and goodness. The rose doesn't have something called beauty curled up inside it, which jumps out into my brain when I go into the garden, and makes me think, 'Ah, there is beauty.' I decide what I like, what looks good to me. I create beauty, and it is perfectly possible that what is beautiful for me is ugly for you. It is the same with goodness and with truth. Neither exists in any way at all, apart from what we each individually create for ourselves.

How do I defend this view? I don't need to. I'm certainly not going to fall into the trap of trying to show that this view of truth is true, since that would be to

accept your traditional concept of truth. All I need to say
is that this way of looking at truth is true for me. I suppose
I ought to stop there, and allow that you others have as
much right to say that your view of truth is true for you.
If you do that, I can't argue with you. But when you start
using your concept of truth to try and show that mine is
inadequate, I have to try and answer on your own terms.
So I have tried to show that all other concepts of truth are
inadequate; and that, in the last analysis, is why I accept
mine.

★   ★   ★

Well, there it is. Five approaches to truth, three of them
holding to the six traditional principles we outlined at the
beginning of the chapter, one totally rejecting them, and
the other somewhere in between.

Do we dare ask which one is right? Or are we back
with the Dodo, and his modern counterpart, Sarah: all are
as right as the others; everybody has won?

I personally believe that none of the five views of the
nature of truth is totally satisfactory, though between them
they contain a great deal of wisdom, and aspects that we
can incorporate into a view of truth that can stand up to
contemporary criticism. We will be coming to that in a
later chapter. But meanwhile we will glance at one
significant point concerning the views represented above
by Alex, Chris, Tom and Mary.

They are all looking for some way of guaranteeing
truth. In each case they come up with an answer: 'Truth is
self-guaranteeing', 'God', 'reason', or 'it works'. Any of
those answers look pretty impressive to start with, and a

good case could be made for each. But it is possible to face all of them with the challenge: 'How do you know that this guarantee is the right one? How do you show that "Truth is self-guaranteeing" is true? Granted that God is a convenient way of guaranteeing truth, how do you show that it is true that God exists? How can you show the truth of "Reason is the test of truth" or "What works is true"?'

The fact is that as soon as anyone makes a statement about truth, it can be challenged by the questions 'Is that statement true?' 'How can you show that it is true?' This applies as much to Sarah as it does to the other four. Despite her insistence that she doesn't have a 'view of truth' like the others, she still makes plenty of statements that claim to be true. 'I don't have a view of truth', 'I do accept pragmatism', 'Truth doesn't come from outside', 'I make truth', and so on. All of these statements make sense only if they are taken as claims to truth. Sarah is saying to Alex and Chris and Tom and Mary that these things are really so. And it is perfectly possible for them to reply 'Are they really so?' – 'Are they true?'

Here, of course, we are at the start of a very slippery slope. It doesn't take much thought to see that if Alex or Sarah or one of the others wishes to stick up for the truth of their basic statements, they can only do so by making some more statements. And then we can challenge the truth of these new statements, and ask for them to be justified. And so on. And so on. For ever.

Maybe there are some people who would enjoy spending the rest of eternity going further and further back in the chain of justification. Most of us have better things to do, and, in any case, we are not inclined to accept the legitimacy of the kind of scepticism this attitude implies. Most of us want to say to the sceptical philosopher who keeps asking 'How do you know you exist?', 'How can you prove that the outside world really is there?', and the like, that we do know, and that is the end of the matter. It is the same with the question of truth. Those who claim that truth is self-guaranteeing, or that God or reason guarantee it, want to come back to the sceptic with, 'We don't need to say any more than that. God is big enough, or reason is clear enough; these things are the explanation; we don't need an infinite chain of explanations.'

That is not to say that Alex and Chris and Tom and Mary aren't able to defend their position, and give good reasons why it is the best out of the five. Any of them will be happy to do so. But there is all the difference in the world between giving good reasons for something, and supplying that logically watertight proof that we were looking at in chapter three, which will for ever silence all the questions of the sceptical philosopher. Asking for that is asking too much, for a very simple reason: issues of truth are not theoretical, like maths and logic. When we are talking about truth, we are talking about the real world, the world as it really is. And in that real world, as we have seen, although various types of proof are perfectly legitimate and function well, the narrow concepts of proof found in maths and logic are not appropriate.

7
Compromise

It is time to tackle the two closely related questions that were raised in the last chapter:

Is truth something outside of us, something authoritative, universal, and eternal, that we discover, submit to, and so on; *or* is it something internal, personal, which we create, 'truth-for-me'?

Is truth fixed, absolute, unchanging; *or* is it all relative, to time, place, person, culture, situation, etc?

The traditional view of truth, as generally understood, went for the first part of each question: truth is outside of us, authoritative, universal, fixed, absolute, and so on. Sarah, on the other hand, and the most significant part of today's culture, choose the second set of alternatives: truth is internal to the individual, changing, relative, and so on. Who is right?

Both and neither. The contemporary reaction to the traditional view is typical of so many reactions: it is over the top. Seeing faults and problems in the traditional approach, it rejects that approach wholesale. It wrongly assumes that to reject, we must reject totally; if the traditional view says truth is outside of us, then it must be inside us; if it says truth is fixed, then truth has to lose all its fixed points.

But if we are looking for Annabella and decide that she is not at the North Pole, we do not have to conclude immediately that she is at the South Pole. She may be there, but there are many other places, somewhere between the North Pole and the South Pole, where she could be. In the same way, there are plenty of intermediate positions between the two extremes: truth can be something complex, with elements that are both outside us and inside us, fixed and changing. If we reject the traditional view we don't have to go to Sarah's extreme.

* * *

Not that Sarah's position isn't attractive. In the first place, in that it allows everybody to hold their own views and accepts them all equally as the truth, it is very tolerant and very generous. Everyone has won, and everyone gets a prize. Most of us are sick of intolerance. We've had enough of dogmatic people who assert their own views and reject everyone else's. We find bigotry and fanaticism distasteful. We recognize that the world is bigger than our backyard, and it contains all sorts of people with all sorts of views. There is no way we can all be fighting each other, insisting that we are right and everyone else is wrong. We've got to learn to accept each other, and allow each other to hold our differing beliefs. Dogmatism is out; tolerance is in. I've got my truth; you have yours.

Secondly, this approach is attractive because it provides a solution to a number of problems. To the old problem: 'How can we be sure we've got the truth?', it answers, 'Because whatever you decide is the truth *is* the truth, for you. You can be absolutely sure of it.' If we ask, 'What about disagreements? How do we sort out conflicting ideas?' it replies, 'You don't need to. You would only need to if there was just one set of truths. But that's not so; there are as many sets of truths as people who think them up.' And if we start asking what is the basis for truth; is it reason, experience, authority, or whatever, its answer is straightforward: none of them is; *you* are the basis; *you* make the truth; you can use your reason or your experience to help you if you like, or you can just create some truth without using either; that is entirely up to you.

Thirdly, those who support this view can point to a number of areas where applying it has been beneficial. It is an approach to truth that really works, they claim. It is like what has happened in ethics. In the old days, when we believed in right and wrong, people were incredibly restricted and repressed; they couldn't do this, they had to do that, and so on. Then they were liberated: there was no right and wrong; each person was able to create their own rules and principles. Suddenly we are all free; the chains are broken; we can be ourselves. So it is, we are told, with truth. People are free now to believe what they like. A religiously inclined person can believe religious things; a person who doesn't want a religion can happily be an atheist. Sally's 'Stone-Age' tribe in Papua New Guinea can be left alone to follow their own beliefs; we don't have to try and make them think the same way as we do. Jenny's history lecturers can each develop their own distinctive interpretations of history, and each get a book published for their pains.

But in spite of all its attractiveness, and although it does work in some areas, this approach to truth will not do. It contains a fatal flaw. We have already seen that in order to hold her view of truth, Sarah has to break her basic principle; if she says, 'I believe truth is something personal, created by each individual', she is stating something that makes sense only if we accept it as an outside-of-us truth: 'Sarah believes truth is personal, etc.' All her beliefs may

109

be, as she claims, internal to her, inside Sarah; but she is asking us to accept something as true that, though it may be inside Sarah, is outside of us.

To put the same point another way, Sarah is saying, 'There is no fixed truth', or, 'All the truths we traditionally thought were fixed and universal and eternal, are relative, changing, and so on.' But in making these statements she herself is doing exactly what she says we may not do: she is stating fixed universal truths. She cannot state her position without contradicting it.

Maybe this doesn't quite demolish her position. Sarah has one final option: she can accept that she cannot state her postition without contradicting it; so she doesn't state it. She doesn't state anything, since even to say, 'I believe roses are beautiful', is as much making a claim to external fixed truth as, 'It is true-for-me that we should all accept everyone's beliefs as true.' So she remains silent. For ever. Taking Sarah's 'truth-for-me' position means not just loss of truth, but loss of communication.

No one who holds Sarah's position has yet managed to be that consistent – so far as I know. But even if we tolerate a measure of inconsistency, we still come up against an insuperable problem. Suppose Sarah is right: truth is personal; what is true-for-me is true; what is true-for-you is equally true, even if it contradicts what is true-for-me. Suppose Iain says, 'Edinburgh is further north than London', and Alison says, 'Edinburgh is further south than London.' According to Sarah's view, both are equally right: it is true-for-Iain that Edinburgh is north of London, and true-for-Alison that it is south. But suppose Iain and Alison meet, and, rather than remaining silent, get into conversation. Iain struggles to understand what Alison is saying; is she meaning something special by the word 'south', for instance? Perhaps she is saying that Edinburgh as a city has a more 'southern' feel to it, or that its climate is more Mediterranean. But no: she insists she means it is geographically further south. Perhaps she isn't referring to London, England, but to a village in the north of Finland which she calls London. No, she means London, England. So Iain produces an atlas and various people who often travel between Edinburgh and London, all of whom support his position. But Alison still insists Edinburgh is south of London, and goes on insisting even after Iain drives her in his car from London to Edinburgh, heading north all the time. Sooner or later Iain will come to the end of his efforts to make sense of what Alison is saying; he will reach the point where her statement is not just untrue-for-him, but meaningless. He has tried every way to understand it, to squeeze some meaning out of it. And he has failed. The statement is meaningless. It says nothing; it is empty. Sarah's approach means loss of truth; and loss of truth, even if we try and pretend it does not mean loss of communication, means loss of meaning.

★ ★ ★

Let's try a bit of compromise. Instead of limiting ourselves to the 'either/or' approach we began the chapter with, let's try a bit of 'both/and.' Cannot truth be in some way both external and internal, both fixed and relative?

Facts and interpretation

Have a look at this picture for a moment. What is it?

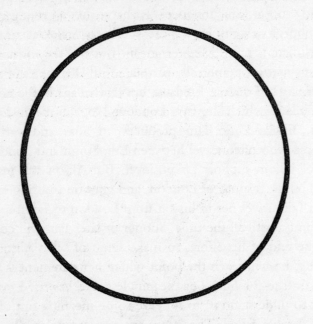

A plate viewed from above? The sun? A circle? Zero? The entrance to a rabbit's burrow? The head of a nail? A mark for a very poor piece of work? The fifteenth letter of the alphabet?

Right every time! And lots of other things there isn't space to list. Dozens of people could say it is dozens of different things, and they would all be right. So we can say: 'It is a plate', 'It is the sun', 'It is a circle', and so on, and all those statements would be true. If you asked enough people with good imaginations, you could have millions of different statements about what it is, and they would all be true.

But suppose someone was to say: 'It's Buckingham Palace.' What then? I guess most of us would think for a bit, check to see if the person is joking, maybe even try squinting in a cross-eyed way and holding the paper at arm's length; but, even if we tolerantly said, 'I accept it is Buckingham Palace for you', we'd have pretty strong reservations. 'The head of a nail, yes; a rabbit's burrow – OK. But Buckingham Palace . . .?'

Now try this one.

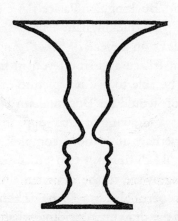

A vase? Two faces? An ornate egg timer? An upside-down candlestick? Some squiggles on a piece of paper? The list isn't so long this time; a few ingenious people might add a few acceptable suggestions, but this drawing doesn't seem to be open to so many possibilities.

And what about this?

C
O
M
P
R
O
M
I
S
E

Right first time: Buckingham Palace. Not the sun, nor a rabbit; nor even Windsor Castle or the Tower of London. A very limited range of possibilities; perhaps just three that we could accept: 'Buckingham Palace'; 'A picture of Buckingham Palace'; 'A Buckingham Palace shaped arrangement of ink marks on a piece of paper'. And if I took you to Buckingham Palace and stood you in front of it, you wouldn't then be able to call it a picture or ink on paper. The only option would be 'Buckingham Palace'.

Seeing what a drawing is may appear very straightforward. But perhaps it is more complex than it seems. Maybe we should distinguish two processes. There is the process of being aware of the drawing, the fact that it is there, and, in particular, its shape. Then there is the interpreting of the drawing, deciding what it is picturing. The first process seems to fit well with the traditional concept of truth; there is something outside of us, something fixed, which we accept. We don't create the drawing; it is there on the page; it would still be there even if we closed the book; even if no one ever reads the book, it would still exist, independently of everyone.

But seeing and accepting the drawing isn't enough. The

second process, that of interpreting it, is a vital part of our coming to know the truth. We are not passive; we contribute to the overall process. We get to work on the drawing, and decide what it is. And that is something that happens inside of us; we do it; we can agree with Sarah that we are being creative.

115

But there is one important point of contrast with Sarah's view. Our creativeness is within limits. We can decide that the first drawing is the sun or the fifteenth letter of the alphabet, but not that it is Buckingham Palace. And when we are presented with more detailed drawings or objects, our options are even more limited. Some things seem to allow us no freedom to be creative at all. We add our interpretation to the experience of standing in front of Buckingham Palace, and the interpretation we add seems to be dictated by what is there; I suppose we could interpret it as a huge cardboard cut-out, or a hallucination; but even then we'd have to say 'a cardboard cut-out (or hallucination) of Buckingham Palace'. Our act of interpretation, internal though it is to us, is directed by the facts that are external to us and beyond our control.

In other areas we seem to have a greater degree of freedom. When we say, 'That tree is a lovely shape' we have added quite a bit of ourselves to the basic statement, 'There is a tree over there.' It is quite open to someone else to say, 'Oh, I don't think it's very special; I don't like the way it gets thin towards the top.' Here we are getting a bit nearer to beautiful-for-me and ugly-for-you; but we are certainly not saying, with Sarah, that we are free to create all the truth that is going about the tree. We work within limits: that the tree is there; it has an agreed shape;

it gets thin towards the top, and so on. The area of freedom is over whether or not thinness towards the top adds or detracts from the tree's beauty. This may well be a significant area of freedom, but it is freedom within well-defined limits.

The degree of freedom we have in adding our personal interpretation to what we are given in our experiences seems to depend on how much clear information we are provided with in the particular area. When we are debating whether or not a tree is lovely, we agree on the fact of the tree's existence, its shape, and so on; but we disagree over whether or not it is lovely because loveliness is a vague concept that we've never got round to defining. In the same way, if we are out walking on a misty day, and see a distant shape, ill-defined and vague, we might well be justified in arguing over whether it is a tree or a bush; but, confronted with a seventy-foot oak tree on a bright sunny day, we hardly have freedom to insist it is a blackberry bush.

We all know the story of the blind men and the elephant, used often by the people who argue that a number of contradictory statements can be true at the same time. One felt the elephant's tail and said the elephant was like a rope; another felt its leg and said the elephant was like a tree; another felt its trunk and said the elephant was like a snake, and so on. Delightful though the story is, it only argues the case of relativists because the amount of information each man had was incredibly limited. For a start they were all blind; then, for some reason, they each only made a very cursory examination of one bit of the elephant. Had they been a bit more thorough, and gathered a bit more information, or even consulted with each other, they would have got a more complete picture, and a much more accurate knowledge of what an elephant really is like. After all, the truth, just one truth, was standing before them.

So the traditional 'scientific' approach has a lot to be said for it. If we are going to arrive at the truth, we don't just make a personal choice, plucking some idea out of the air, and then claiming this is truth-for-me. Rather, we gather as much relevant information as we can; we observe carefully, and check our observations with others. True, we add our interpretation, but we don't just add any interpretation; we select the one that fits all the details.

So there are definite limits to our freedom to create truth. It is limited to the area of our interpretation; we don't create the basic drawing or our experiences of the world around us; and even the interpretation is generally severely limited by the content of the experience. Research scientists have the freedom to invent an interpretation of the data they are investigating, though it has to be an interpretation that fits the data; if they start changing the data to fit their interpretation they will soon be in trouble. The religious person has the freedom to produce a God-centred interpretation of the world, and the atheist has the freedom to produce a Godless one. But neither of them have the freedom to decide what does or does not go to make up the world. They both have to accept a vast number of things as given, and then seek to show that their interpretation fits the facts. This is a point we will be picking up later.

★ ★ ★

So we are asking to have our cake and eat it. We don't want to be forced to an extreme; we refuse to accept that truth must be either wholly outside of us or wholly inside of us, either wholly fixed or totally relative. Truth is complex; though we may well wish to say that for the most part it exists quite independently of us, and is in some senses unchanging and eternal, we still want to say that, within certain limits, we can affect it and help shape it.

There is a snag with this position that has often been pointed out by those who want to go to the kind of extreme that Sarah has adopted. If we say that any given truth can be part external and fixed, and part (however small a part) internal and so affected by us, we can never be sure of any truth. Allow just one little bit of uncertainty in, they say, and the whole becomes uncertain; even if there are ninety-nine good strong links in a chain, one broken one will ruin the lot.

There are several answers we could make to this. We could point out that *it is based on an inappropriate concept of certainty.* It seems to assume that to know any truth we have to have a 100% logically proved case, that allows for no element of doubt at all. But we have seen in chapter three that this is not so. It is not the way we operate in real life, whatever we may do when proving mathematical theorems or truths of logic.

A second answer is to point out that *it is usually possible to distinguish the aspects of a truth that are based on something outside of us, and the aspects that we personally have contributed.*

If I'm in London at supper time with a yen to walk down Princes Street and I say, 'Sadly, Edinburgh is too far north of London to go there for an evening out', most people would have no problem accepting that this statement covers at least three aspects, two of which are external, and one of which is personal to me: 'Edinburgh is north of **119** London', 'It is too far to go from London to Edinburgh for an evening out', and 'It is sad that this is so.' The third is a personal comment and can quite legitimately be a matter of debate; the first two cannot be, since they are governed by geography and the availability of Concorde. I am perfectly entitled to claim certainty over Edinburgh's whereabouts and the time it takes to get there, while allowing that the 'sadly' bit is debatable; my wife may be delighted that we can't go there for the evening, since she wants to get an early night.

A third thing to remember is that *the scope for our personal contribution in many areas is very limited indeed or even non-existent.* Once the mist has cleared and the seventy-foot oak tree has been examined and certified by a team of experts, we simply do not have the option to say that it is a blackberry bush. If we are using the words 'blackberry bush' in their generally accepted sense, we cannot apply them to the oak tree; the facts of the situation prevent us.

So the objection that we lose certainty if we allow that sometimes truths can contain both external and internal elements is not valid. We can be still claim certainty in the areas where it is applicable, while allowing that some elements of our claims may be open to debate. This takes us back to the point we raised at the beginning of this chapter about tolerance. We all dislike intolerance, but there are plenty of areas where tolerance is totally inappropriate. If we set out from London on a flight to Edinburgh and after ten minutes the flight crew tolerantly announce that some think Edinburgh is just a quarter of an hour from London, so they are going to land the aircraft now, we would have cause for alarm, especially as there is no airport handy. Scientists cannot be tolerant over whether the boiling point of water is 100° or 200°. Granted, polite scientists may still concede that if someone wants to insist that water boils at 200° they're not going to stop them, though if we're on the flight to Edinburgh about to land in the fields of Buckinghamshire we may be justified in being less than polite. But being polite towards someone with whom you disagree is not the same as allowing that their belief is as much the truth as your belief.

8
Reason

I once spent a couple of weeks camping on the shore of an estuary near Mombasa. Each day I would swim out to a raft anchored some distance from the shore and lie watching the brightly coloured fish in the clear water below me. I was quite content with watching, but every now and then a couple of fishermen would come along the shore carrying a large net. They would wade into the water, cleverly cast the net, wait, and pull it up. The fish had seen it all before, and few of them got caught.

If we can judge by one of Jesus' parables, fish in first century Palestine weren't so canny. The fishermen in the story used this method and caught a whole net full of all sorts of fish. After pulling the net to the shore they sat down on the beach, collected the good fish into baskets, and threw the bad fish away.

That's our policy for the next couple of chapters. We are going to cast a net in the hope of finding some reasonably positive concepts of truth. Then we'll try to sorting them out, keeping whatever seems useful, and throwing the rest away.

★ ★ ★

Truth is . . . living

We'll start by going back the best part of three thousand years. Not this time to the ancient Greeks, but to a people whose culture was well developed long before Greek civilization – the ancient Hebrews. Their distinctive insight into the nature of truth can best be expressed by contrasting it with the Greek view; although Hebrew thought has had a great deal of influence on the development of Western ideas, the Greek concept of truth was more influential; so, even today, the Hebrew concept still may strike us as strange. In contrasting the two views, we need to remember that there was a good deal of overlap between them. Nevertheless the primary emphasis of each is very different.

For the Greeks truth belonged to the mind; it was to be put in the same category as reason, intellect, thought, and ideas. For the Hebrews truth belonged to life; it was to be lived; if it was to be put in any category, it belonged with words like righteousness, justice and love. Greeks believed the truth; Hebrews did the truth. Greeks contemplated the truth, and the act of contemplation left both contemplator and contemplated much as they were before; Hebrews got involved with truth, entered into a relationship with it, and were shaped and changed in the process. For Greeks truth was static and detached; for the Hebrews it was dynamic and personal.

The Hebrews' dynamic concept of living truth was, of course, closely linked to their concept of God. Long before Jesus said, 'I am the truth', the Old Testament was claiming that truth was to be found primarily in God, not just in what he is, but in what he does, in speaking, in the covenant relationship he established, in his faithfulness, in his righteous acts, even in his judgment as he applied true standards to the nations. Our truth, the truth of our human lives, is founded and patterned on his truth. However much we may claim to know the truth, unless our lives are righteous, demonstrating the truth, and putting God's will into action, we are in reality far from truth.

Here we have an original approach to the nature of truth, one not influenced in any way by the Greek concept that has tended to dominate much of the history of our culture. It offers us maybe four specific insights: 125

1. Truth is primarily to be lived, not believed.
2. Truth itself is alive and dynamic, not static.
3. Truth is rooted in God.
4. Truth that is intellectually known but not put into practice is untruth.

It is interesting to speculate what would have happened if the Christian church had retained these particular Hebrew concepts instead of allowing the Greek concept of truth to dominate so much of its thinking. Perhaps there would have been more stress on Christianity as something we live rather than something we believe; truth would have been seen primarily in terms of a way and a life rather than as creeds or sets of doctrines. As things worked out, the fact that the New Testament was written in Greek, and that its defenders had to seek ways of making it acceptable to a culture saturated with ideas rooted in Greek philosophy, made it almost inevitable that the Greek concept should predominate.

★ ★ ★

Perhaps, as you read about the Hebrew idea of doing the truth, you were reminded of the view of Mary Praxis in chapter six. She was prepared to settle for a short-term form of truth; what is true today won't necessarily be true tomorrow. But tied in with it were a couple of elements that are worth looking at. 'Let's get on with living,' she said. 'If we can live with something, if it works, if it is fruitful in discovering things and doing things, let's take it as a kind of working truth.' Apart from the concepts of working truth or permanent truth, the two elements are living truth or living with truth, and truth working or being fruitful.

It is not too difficult to think of some things that are unliveable, or situations we could not live with. We come across some of them in dreams, and others in books about philosophy. We couldn't live in a world, for example, where there is no consistency, where everything changes all the time. We go to walk through a door, and it changes into a wall; we put a grape into our mouth and it becomes a lion. But, equally, we couldn't live in a world where nothing changed at all. We wouldn't be able to walk through the door, since we couldn't change our position. We couldn't eat a grape, since the grape must remain unchanged for ever. We wouldn't even be able to think, since our brain cells and ideas must remain unchanged.

So, given a criterion that truth must be liveable, we can conclude that it must be true that the world we live in contains both consistency and change. We might want to add that most things are consistent most of the time, and that even change has elements of consistency about it; it doesn't happen randomly, for no reason, but according to fairly predictable patterns. I change my position, but trees don't normally change theirs. And if I want to go into the garden, it is fairly predictable that I will go through the door.

It doesn't seem too difficult, however, to think of things that are unliveable, that we couldn't live with, and yet that are or could be true. Billions of years ago, we are told, the earth was such that no life existed, or was even possible. A nuclear holocaust destroying the whole earth wouldn't exactly be liveable, but, sadly, it could be true. Perhaps we need to define our concept of 'liveable' a little more carefully. We need to move away from 'something that I could happily live with' to 'something that I can conceive of happening, whether I like the idea or not'. It is a question of living with the concept, rather than living with the actuality. I can live with the concept that billions of years ago the temperature on the surface of the earth was thousands of degrees, even though I wouldn't have lasted long if I'd been there.

So if we modify Mary's suggestion in this way, we seem to have a useful idea: what is true must be liveable or liveable with, at least as a concept. What if we turn it round the other way: what is liveable is true? Here at once we are in trouble. Millions of people will feel that winning £5 million on the National Lottery is something they could very happily live with, but it can never be true that millions will win that amount. So we have to be a little careful in applying the principle that 'truth is something you can live or live with', and make sure we get it the right way round.

The second element mentioned by Mary is that truth should work, or be fruitful. Again, this is a practical concept, linking the idea of action in with the idea of truth. But the activity it refers to is a special kind of activity or action; it is not something pointless, like waves

127

beating for ever on the shores of the sea. At the back of Mary's mind is a machine at work, turning out computers, or a system of farming producing food, or a scientific theory which helps us develop further technology.

An obvious question we could ask is: 'Working or fruitful for whom, or for what?' What is fruitful for the fisherman can hardly be said to be fruitful for the fish. Mary clearly meant 'fruitful for the human race', since she defined it in terms of discovering things and doing things. That fits well with her 'short-term truth'; the view Mary represents has often (though not always) been associated with short-term benefit for the human race or, rather, Western industrialized society, without much thought for anything else. But if we are looking for something more long-term and more universal we might have to cast our net rather wider. We would need to talk of long-term or ultimate benefit, and apply the definition not just to ourselves, nor even to the whole human race, but to other creatures that share Planet Earth with us, to the environment, to the planet itself. Maybe even that is too parochial, and we should go further and speak in terms of the ultimate benefit of the universe. Perhaps we shouldn't even stop there, but should take the last step and anchor our concept of truth in the will of God.

You may have noticed that as we have discussed this concept of truth as what works or is fruitful, we have almost strayed into the area of what is right and good. Indeed, there doesn't seem to be anything to choose between: 'Truth is what is fruitful for the environment or planet Earth' and: 'Truth is what is right for the environment' or: 'Truth is what is good for Planet Earth'.

Traditionally thinkers have not been at all keen on crossing over from 'true' to 'right' and 'good' in this way. 'Truth' has been thought of as the domain of science and maybe philosophy; it has to do with hard facts. 'Goodness' and 'rightness' are a different sort of thing; they belong to the area of morals and ethics, where there are no hard facts, and everything is very fuzzy.

But it's possible that in taking this attitude traditional thinkers have been wrong, and too quick to divide the world into clearly separated areas. Again, we are casting our net wide. Perhaps we are going to need to incorporate concepts of rightness and goodness into our concept of truth to make it strong enough and rich enough for all it needs to be able to cover.

Before we leave Mary's concept of truth we can note that turning the second of its elements round is no better than turning the first one round. 'What works is true' is a motto that many people have adopted. But it doesn't take much effort to think of all sorts of things that can be said to work or to be fruitful, but are not true. I'm not thinking so much of lies or forgeries or the like that are certainly not true, though many would claim they work, or are fruitful. Since we, unlike Mary, are interested in the long term rather than the short term, it could be argued that in the long run such things don't work and are not fruitful. 'Cheats never prosper' was a saying that was around when I was young; I didn't see a great deal of evidence for its truth then, but I suppose if you believe in a Day of Judgment you can say that lies and the like don't ultimately work. But we are on safer ground with, say, J.R.R. Tolkien's Middle Earth, an imaginary world where

everything fits and works and could be said to be fruitful –
but none of it is true.

★ ★ ★

Truth is . . . what everyone agrees about

It is tempting to link truth with agreement. If I say
starlings are gawky, and you agree, and the neighbours
agree and the president of the Royal Society for the
Protection of Birds agrees, we're inclined to say, 'That's
settled then; starlings are gawky'. Sadly, this view is easily
demolished. There was a time when everyone agreed the
earth was flat. We can question what we mean by agreement; how many have to agree? Is it you and me and a
few others, or 51% of the population, or the vast majority,
or absolutely everybody? Besides, in many areas agreement isn't as easy to come by as we might think, and even
when we've got it, it doesn't last. Somebody is bound to
object to calling starlings gawky; The Flat Earth Society
still has members. Even if people agree now, we can't be
sure they will still agree in ten years' time. We have learnt
to be very cautious of statements like, 'Scientists agree that
. . .' or, 'The assured results of modern scholarship tell us
. . .' or, 'Every schoolboy knows . . . .'

Again, we can try turning the phrase around. Instead of
saying, 'What we agree is true', in the sense that if
something is agreed by us all then it must be true, we can
try, 'What is true will be agreed', in the sense that if
something is true, we will agree to it. This doesn't seem to
help much; the only way we might salvage something

from it is to add: ' - if we have sufficient information' or 'ultimately'. If the day ever comes when we are all free from bias, all aware of relevant information, all willing to think through the implications, and so on, then, hopefully, the truth will stare us each in the face, and we will agree.

131

★   ★   ★

Truth is . . . self-evident

Talking of truth staring us in the face leads us to another concept of truth that was touched on by Alex in chapter six, and has been picked up by thinkers and philosophers from time to time: truth is something that is self-evident. There is something about truth that enables us to recognize it when we see it. Maybe it is like pleasure or pain. It can come from many different sources, taking all sorts of forms; but when it comes we know it for what it is. We don't need persuasion or proof that pain is pain; there is something about pain, and something about us, that makes recognition instant and infallible. So with truth; there is something in it and something in us that enables us to recognize it when it comes. For Alex that 'something' in us was the divine spark of reason. Later thinkers used the concept that we are made in the image of God, and a good God would not let us be deceived.

That truth is self-evident is a concept that works well in certain areas, but not so well in others. There certainly does appear to be something self-evident about '3 + 1 = 4', or about 'A bachelor is an unmarried man.'

We could make a case for self-evident truth in statements like: 'Trees that we and others keep seeing and bumping into really are there', or 'Something must have made that door slam', or 'Tomorrow today will be yesterday'. But what about 'The village of Ruan Minor is on the Lizard Peninsula' ? Most people would not find that self-evident, however true it may be. Granted, it is self-evident to the inhabitants of Ruan Minor, and to people who are fortunate enough to know their way round the Lizard. And perhaps the advocates of this approach to truth will claim that that is sufficient to show that it is a self-evident truth. Life is too short for all of us to take on board all truth. Most people don't need to know where Ruan Minor is; for those who do, the fact that it is on the Lizard is a self-evident truth.

Even if we concede that one, it still isn't too difficult to think of things that could be true, but don't seem to be self-evident. 'The defendant killed the victim' could well be true, but the need for a trial and evidence and prosecution and defence and judge and jury seems to make it quite clear that it is not self-evident.

The most we can claim, I suggest, in this area of self-evidence, is that some truths appear to be self-evident to just about everybody; and some truths are not at all self-evident to most people, but they may be to a limited number who are most personally concerned. It is self-evident to me that my wife loves me, though it certainly is not so to the billions of people who have never met either of us. We could even say that the truth of the defendant killing the victim is self-evident to the defendant, and maybe even, in some sense, to the victim, however obscure it may be to the jury.

* * *

The truth is . . . what is beyond doubt

Some have suggested a criterion for truth closely related to the idea of self-evidence: that something is true if it is beyond doubt. '3 + 1 = 4'; 'I think, therefore I am', and, 'The writer of this book is called Peter' are true because no one doubts them. 'The M25 motorway is the world's largest car park' or 'The Tories have made a great contribution to the well-being of Britain' cannot be accepted as true, because there are people who would doubt their truth. One snag with this criterion is that such a test would leave us with very little truth. We only need to have one doubter to destroy any given truth, and, one way or another, sceptical philosophers (and others) have been able to doubt just about everything, including their own existence.

Perhaps, however, we feel a bit impatient about sceptical philosophers holding us all to ransom, and would want to soften the criterion a little to 'what most people do not doubt'. Sadly, this falls to the flat earth objection.

Maybe the biggest problem with this kind of approach is that it seems to remove the criterion for truth from things in the world around us and place it inside of us. It claims that a thing is true if lots of people feel sure about it. But if I say I am sure of something I am telling you about my psychological state, not about the thing I'm referring to. 'I'm sure I put the keys back in my pocket' informs you about how I'm feeling, not where the keys are. Though most of us feel that our psychological state of being sure is often the result of our having found the truth, we would be very hesitant to say that our sense of assurance is the basis of something's being true. We want truth to be more that just our state of mind; we want it to be anchored in something outside of us.

★ ★ ★

Truth is . . . what we have good evidence for

This leads us to a very different approach. Many have felt that the key to establishing truth is the amount of evidence that is available to support it. If John claims to be a train driver, and his wife backs him up, and he produces documentary evidence that he has passed all the relevant exams, and we see him at the local station seated at the controls of the 9.25, then we conclude his claim is true. On the other hand, if his wife tells you he is just fantasizing and that his real job is accountancy, and the local firm of accountants say he works full time with them, and when taken to the station he has difficulty telling the front end of the train from the back, the counter-evidence would seem sufficient to make us conclude his claim is false. If the evidence on either side is roughly balanced or if there simply isn't enough to make a decision on, we suspend judgment or make a qualified commitment: 'I think he probably is a train driver', 'I'm fairly sure he's not', and so on, allowing the amount of evidence to determine the level of truth.

As you might expect, the standard objection to this approach is that we can never be sure we've got enough evidence to say that any given thing is true. We are back to the Society for the Propagation of Goldfish again. A lifetime's work showing that all black goldfish turn gold can be demolished by one elderly black specimen. But our 135 discussions in chapters two and three might make us reluctant to give way to this objection. Whatever the sceptics may say, we do reach the point where we feel we have enough evidence. What constitutes 'enough evidence' will vary from one situation to another; we do not need to have logically watertight proof to decide that last night's ghost was in fact a towel hanging on the line; to try and impose a uniform criterion for proof over every area of truth is a mistake. Further, we do not have to wait until every conceivable possibility of error has been excluded before we can say that something is true. Life is short, and our abilities to investigate are limited. It is just conceivable that we are dreaming, or that the earth is flat after all, but we are not going to let that infinitely remote possibility rob us of the concept of truth, any more than we stop eating because there is a remote possibility someone has put arsenic in our sandwiches.

So here is a concept of truth which focuses on what is outside of us more than on what is inside us. Our inner conviction plays a part, telling us, say, when we have sufficient evidence; but our conviction depends on things that are external to us, things in the world around us like John's wife's statement, his exam certificate, and so on.

* * *

TRUTH: COULD IT BE TRUE?

The last couple of ways of understanding truth we have looked at, seeing truth as something we cannot doubt, or something we have good evidence for, have been explored very thoroughly by those who have followed the rationalistic way of viewing the world that has dominated our culture since the start of the Age of Reason. This brings us back to Tom Brain, whom we met in chapter six, with his clarion call of 'Reason shall be our guide'. The last few decades have seen a strong reaction, maybe overreaction, against this view. Some of it arises from the fear that the science and technology built on this principle is leading our planet into a wasteland; much of it comes from the realization that philosophically it simply does not work, however beneficial its products may have been. Books have been written seeking to show that even scientists do not make their discoveries by means of reason, at any rate in the generally accepted sense. But perhaps the most significant source of the reaction against the total dominance of reason is the awareness that though reason may be a real and significant part of human personhood, it is by no means the only part. We are more than brains or computers; we reason - yes; but we also fear, hope, feel pain, love, enjoy things, relate to one another, and so on. So why should we cry, 'Reason shall be our guide'? Why not, 'Love shall be our guide', or, 'Goodness shall be our guide', or even, 'A careful balance of all the elements that go to make up human personhood shall be our guide'?

Discussions of truth have tended to ignore these less intellectual elements of human persons; perhaps this is because much of the discussing has been done by intellectuals. But if we are seeking to cast our net wide we need to include them in our discussion, and that is what we shall be doing in the next chapter.

137

9
Persons

The shop assistant got my change wrong, and excused herself by saying she didn't feel well: 'I think I've got a touch of 'flu; my brain's not working. You don't get far without a brain.' I tried to be sympathetic, but couldn't resist the comment, 'Oh, I don't know; I can think of several people who have got a long way without any sign of using their brain at all'.

I doubt whether that was much comfort to her; but it is a fact that as humans we don't operate solely on the level of our intellects or reason. We are more than brains; when we've explored and understood everything there is to know about our reason, we've only just begun to explore the rich complexity of what it means to be human.

In my way of seeing things, we are not a set of clearly segregated parts, with, say, our intellect operating in one corner, our feelings in another, and our experiences in another. We are integrated people, and all the different aspects of us are closely interwoven. They work together, and each affects the others.

No one has yet produced a definitive analysis of the different aspects that make up the complex whole that is human personhood. We will pick out five aspects that may have bearing on our search for concepts that will help us get to the heart of the nature of truth.

★ ★ ★

Truth and experience

We have already mentioned several times our ability to receive experiences, of seeing a tree, bumping into a wall, hearing a voice and so on. Experiencing such things is not in itself an operation of our reason; experiences seem to come unbidden and offer themselves to us for the taking; we don't have to think them up or think them through. Granted, our reason frequently gets to work as soon as the experience arrives, making sense of it, fitting it into the whole picture, understanding and responding to the words that are spoken. But experiencing is different from reasoning.

We have also said that most people find direct personal experience very convincing; if we want a source of truth, this is a good one to explore. 'I saw it with my own eyes'; 'I distinctly heard him sound his horn', 'If you don't believe there's a wall there, just try walking through it' – it is hard to argue with these. We could go a stage further, and risk making a claim that our experiences are always true; they always give us the truth. If error creeps in, as we have to admit it sometimes does, it creeps in at the next stage, that of our reason getting to work on the experience. We have an experience of a towel blowing in the wind at night; the experience in itself is totally truthful: a white shape moving in the darkness; but our interpretation of it is wrong; we think it is a ghost.

To claim that experience is always reliable, and that it is our reason as it interprets that experience that makes the mistakes, is to turn the tables on the dominant Age of Reason view that reason alone has the right to judge all things, and does so in a way we can trust. But it is certainly a possible way of looking at things.

There is one specific reason why we tend to put high truth value on the things we experience. It is because they are consistent; they fit together; when our reason gets to work on them they do make sense. Our experiences aren't a random mass of visual images, sounds, and the like, presenting themselves to us in an incoherent jumble, with no system or pattern. They are consistent; we have the experience of seeing a tree; we look away and look back, 143 and the experience of seeing the tree is repeated; we can do this hundreds of times, and each time the experience of that tree happens when we look at that place. We hear the sound of the wind in its branches; we try using touch, and feel the rough bark just where our visual experience tells us the tree is; the various types of experience confirm one another. We experience other trees; they are different in some ways, but their differences all fit into an overall pattern. Our experience of other things, like birds and clouds, also follow a consistent pattern, and the whole sum of our experiences makes up a coherent integrated whole. We consult with others, and find that, given the same circumstances, they experience the same thing. 'Look over there; can you see what I see?' It can't be that I'm imposing my ideas or consistent pattern on the experiences, since you and thousands of others, uninfluenced by me, have the same experiences.

★ ★ ★

Truth and relationship

A second aspect of what it means to be human is *relating*. In a sense everything can be said to be in any number of relationships: Edinburgh is in relationship with Cardiff and

Mount Everest; the moon is in relationship with the earth and the American flag planted in its dust by James Irwin; yesterday has a relationship with tomorrow and the middle of next week. But we might think of these as pretty passive relationships; Everest would be much the same if Edinburgh did not exist, and the flag isn't exactly revolutionizing the moon. Many of my relationships are equally uninteresting; I must be someone's great-great-grandson; I may even be somebody's double; but neither of these relationships are particularly meaningful, nor do they appear to accomplish anything.

Much more significant are the specifically personal relationships in which we are involved, and which seem to lie near the centre of what it means to be human. Our richest relationships, of course, are with other persons. There will be those who are close to us, whom we know well: members of our family whom we love; friends whose company we enjoy; colleagues we work with or bosses we obey; other relationships are real, if slightly less close: muggers we fear, shop assistants we chat to, television news readers we like.

Our relationships aren't limited to other human beings. Maybe as a projection from our relationship with friends and the like, we relate in a more or less personal way to pets and animals, and in a way that is less personal but not wholly impersonal to a variety of objects and situations.

It isn't easy to analyze just what we mean when we say that we relate in a personal way, but I suggest one of the elements is that we are affected or changed in some way by the things or persons we are relating to; and, in richer relationships, they are affected or changed by us. I can choose to ignore somebody; but if I choose to relate to them, to a greater or lesser extent I open myself to them, and allow them to affect me, to give me joy or sorrow, to interest or bore me, to stimulate me to fear or to anger or compassion or whatever. I don't pass them by; nor do I just experience them; I react to them, and am changed as a result; in most cases they react to me, and they too are changed. When we are relating to something that is non-personal, this element of being changed is still there, though only in a one-way direction. On a country walk, I stride on ignoring the scenery; but then a particular view strikes me; I stop, take it in, let it affect me; a beech wood full of bluebells, or a row of crude pylons marching down a valley, giving me pleasure, annoying me.

145

Relating, then, means involvement, being affected, reacting; it is a choice not to pass by or ignore. It is closely linked with experiencing; but where, in experiencing, we pictured the various experiences as coming to us un-bidden and us as simply receiving them, in relating we are choosing to open ourselves up to the person or object in a fuller way, allowing them to affect and change us.

How does this link with the concept of truth? Could it give us a model? Truth can be experienced in an imper-sonal way; it can come to us, but we ignore it or pass it by. But sometimes we relate to it; we engage with it; we open up ourselves to it; we let it affect us, giving us joy or sorrow, stimulating us to compassion or anger or fear; it changes us. All this happens because we are persons, and are able to relate not just to other persons, but to objects and to truth itself.

At their best relationships are strong and deep; they can be developed as time passes, becoming secure, with a high level of commitment. We have already seen in chapter five that as we build a system of beliefs our commitment to them, although present from the start, becomes stronger as those beliefs are tested, challenged, and confirmed over a period of time; so much so that even apparent counter-evidence will not readily shake us. Commitment, in this sense, whether in a relationship or to a set of beliefs, is certainly not blind; it is no leap in the dark; it has a firm base and it is well justified; so it can be very strong.

★   ★   ★

Truth and love

Can we go one stage further, and add love to our list of the elements that make up the complex whole that is human personhood? Certainly there is an element of progression here: from experience to relationship to love. We could justifiably claim that love is relationship at its richest and fullest and best. We could also make a case for love being the deepest need of human beings, and the best hope, if not the only hope, of sorting out the mess the world is in.

None of us would deny the significance of love. But we may feel that it has little to do with the nature of truth. Few recent philosophers have bothered to turn their attention to the subject, and the scientists' interest in it has been very strictly limited. When we are exploring the nature of truth, talk of love could be dismissed as special pleading. Why should the deep needs of human hearts have anything to do with the ultimate character of the universe?

Special pleading or not, we could make two or three points in answer to this. For centuries there has been an assumption underlying all modern knowledge: that a specific element found in human persons is the key that unlocks the door of the whole universe. That element was, of course, reason. Some people tell us that reason is now discredited; but whether this is the case or not, it is open to us to claim that reason is not the only foundational element in human persons, and maybe not the most significant. Love is there as well, and needs to be taken into account. At the very least, could we not try to see if love is a key that fits the door? Secondly, we could point out that, as we have been seeing, our experience of the universe includes a strange and inexplicable feature. There is a pattern, a coherence, a consistency to it all. This isn't something we impose on the world; it is something we find there. Is it too imaginative to see this coherence as a non-personal expression of love, a harmony, a belonging together, fitting together, and working together, each part supporting and fulfilling the other?

If we are attracted to this kind of idea, we shall find ourselves in very good company. Though modern thinkers have been strongly committed to the very impersonal clockwork machine image of the universe, and have bent over backwards to exclude anything that smacks of the personal, older thinkers had no problems in incorporating love as an integral part of their understanding of the universe. The Greek philosopher, Plato, for example, some four hundred years before Jesus Christ, suggested that love is foundational to our discovery of truth. Plato describes a process: we see someone or something that attracts us; they attract us because, in one form or another, they contain beauty or other enriching qualities. As our love goes out to them, we are in effect responding in love to the beautiful, the good, and so on. And, for Plato, when we encounter and respond to these, we are grasping the nature of ultimate reality, and thus knowing ultimate truth. It is significant that the word 'philosophy', coined by the ancient Greeks, does not mean 'knowledge of wisdom' but 'love of wisdom'. The philosopher is primarily one who loves.

But what about the contemporary idea that love is not interested in the truth? Love, we are told, is a feeling; feelings are random, irrational, unpredictable; any causes they may have are 'chance' causes, bearing no justifiable relationship with their object: I love primroses because I associate them with the end of winter, which I dislike; I love my wife because our hormones just happened to be in the right state the first time we met, and so on. Love, they say, is blind.

I don't believe this. There may be some senses in which love is blind; part of the expression of Mary's love for John is that she is unable to see his faults which seem pretty glaring to everyone else. But this love Mary feels for John is only a very limited sort of love, little more than infatuation; and though infatuation contains elements of love, it most certainly is not the full rich thing we call true love. Maybe one day Mary and John will marry; then, as time goes by, the infatuation element may grow less.

John's faults will in time become as clear to Mary as to other people. And it is at that point that the reality of Mary's love is put to the test. If she really loves him, we say, she'll stick with him, faults and all. Real love is love that sees, and still loves.

So awareness of truth and love are far from incompat- **149** ible; instead, knowledge of the truth about the person loved would seem to be foundational for some of the richer forms of love.

There are doubtless many ways of defining love, and many elements that are involved in it. We've already mentioned harmony, belonging together, fitting together, working together, and a mutual supporting and fulfilling. For me a key concept in love is that of enriching, well-being, and wholeness.

Many of the things I love are objects or experiences or activities − or whatever − where the love relationship would seem to be largely one-way. I love them − primroses, Saint-Saëns' piano concertos, and swimming − but they don't love me. Nevertheless they do something for me, and the best way I can describe what they do is to say they enrich me, they contribute to my well being as a person, they make me a more whole person. Conversely, if I claim to love something, it would seem strange if I wanted to destroy it − if I wanted to tear primroses to pieces, attack Saint-Saëns' piano concertos in a musical journal, or campaign for a ban on swimming. Rather, I would want to do what I could to further the well-being of the things I love − support the ban on picking or digging up wild primroses, encourage performances of the concertos, and so on.

Where love is a two-way personal relationship, the element of enriching and furthering the well-being of the person loved is seen even more clearly. John loves Mary. It could, of course, be a wholly selfish love in which he treats her simply as an object, greedy for all that she can contribute to his well-being, but not interested in hers. But love like that, we feel, is very far short of true love. If he has real love for her, he will be deeply concerned for her well-being, to care for her, to enrich her, and so on.

Love, then, is concerned with enriching and well being and wholeness. Tied in with this central concept are other elements closely associated with love: things like acceptance, affirmation, security, and belonging. All of these can have a profound bearing on the concept of truth; in particular, the image of truth as something that enriches us and promotes our well-being and wholeness would seem to be a useful one to explore. Additionally, we might feel there is some mileage in drawing a parallel with the two-way aspect contained in love. Truth, perhaps, is both something that contributes to my wholeness, and something to whose wholeness I can contribute. These are ideas we will be returning to in due course.

* * *

Truth and will

Another aspect of human personhood that greatly interested older thinkers, but which has been rather out of fashion more recently, is that of the will. However hard it may be to define, we are aware that we exercise our wills

in all sorts of ways and at all sorts of levels. Much of the
time, perhaps, our wills are reasonably dormant; we hear
sounds, we see things, and so on, without any effort on
our part; they just happen to us; we are receiving the
sounds or the light waves in a way little different from the
way a microphone or a camera lens might pick them up. 151
But then we hear something that interests us; we turn our
attention to it; we focus in on it; we concentrate; we make
a special effort to follow it or understand it, or whatever.
Something is happening here beyond the capacity of the
microphone or camera.

In the same way, some of our actions appear pretty
involuntary: we breathe, or digest our food, or blink our
eyes, without thinking about it, or making any effort. But
much of what we do requires will-power. We choose to
do things; we set our minds on something; we take
deliberate steps; we make a conscious effort. Here, again,
there seems to be some element present in human persons
that we don't find, say, in a computer, however much
some of our mental processes may seem to parallel the
workings of a computer.

For hundreds of years there have been debates about
how free our wills are; the official dogma of much of our
materialistic culture is that they are not free at all, though
very few people find that possible to accept in practice.
Most of us accept that, within certain limits, we can make
free choices; I can choose to have cornflakes or grapefruit
for breakfast; I can choose to concentrate on my studies,
or let my mind wander.

What bearing might this concept of will and choice
have on our understanding of the nature of truth? Some

thinkers have suggested that its influence is very considerable, even to the extent of claiming that through our wills we actually create truth: I decide what I want to be true, and in a creative act of will, I make that the truth for me. Others have gone to the opposite extreme and suggested that our wills are dormant in the reception of truth: truth comes to us and we accept it without any action on our part. Others have felt that our wills are active, to a greater or lesser degree, not so much in creating truth, but in deciding which alternative candidates for truth we wish to adopt, and also in the element of commitment to the one we do adopt. This view ties in with some of the things we were looking at in chapter five.

* * *

Truth and goodness

Our discussion in chapter eight of truth as what works or is fruitful ended up, perhaps surprisingly, by suggesting there may be a close link between truth and rightness or goodness. This was because we felt that Mary Praxis' suggestion was helpful but too narrow. Truth has got to be more than what works or is fruitful simply for Western industrialized society. We wanted to expand it as widely as possible: fruitful for the whole human race, for the environment, for Planet Earth, for the whole of the universe, and maybe even for God. But, in this context, 'what is fruitful' and 'what is good' and 'what is right' appear interchangeable.

This ties in with another essential element of human personhood: we are morally responsible beings. Despite

Lizzie's arguments in chapter one, most people find it impossible to live without assuming that there are some fixed points of goodness and badness, rightness and wrongness. Again, our existing together in society depends on the concept of such fixed points. Discussion for most people centres not around whether or not we should have such fixed points, but rather on how we decide which fixed points to adopt, and how we know we've got the right ones once we have adopted them. Perhaps not surprisingly, these discussions sound very similar to the discussions about truth. Some say goodness and rightness are immediately self-evident; others say they are decided by majority agreement; others define them in terms of what works, bringing about the greatest happiness of the greatest number, and so on. In other words, the suggested criteria for rightness and goodness are much the same as those for truth. 153

Can we conclude, then, that truth is closely related to rightness and goodness, and that the contemporary chasm between what is factually true and what is morally right should be done away with? Certainly if we asked the ancient Greeks or the ancient Hebrews they would have replied Yes. The Greeks saw truth and goodness virtually merging as the ultimate form of what is real; the Hebrews, with their practical emphasis, saw truth as what the good person does. The fact that these views have long been out of fashion does not necessarily mean that they are to be rejected; it may be well worth our while to keep an open mind.

★ ★ ★

TRUTH: COULD IT BE TRUE?

In this chapter we have listed five aspects of what it means to be a human person: the ability to experience things, the ability to relate, to love, to exercise will, and to be morally aware. I'm sure the list is incomplete; and, of course, we have to add from the previous chapter the aspect that modern thought has stressed to the exclusion of all else: the ability to reason. As I said at the beginning, it is probably unwise to try and categorize or compartmentalize them in any strict way. We are complex but integrated beings; human personhood is a whole, not merely a collection of parts. Our interest in exploring these aspects has been to see if they have any bearing on the nature of truth; one way and another, each of them seems to have given us something of a clue; we have cast our net wide, and have caught some interesting fish. In the next chapter, our aim will be to sit down on the seashore and begin to sort the mixed bag of the last two chapters into some sort of helpful order.

10
Testing

Here we are, then, back on the beach. We've done our fishing, and a nice mixed lot we've caught. The first thing to do is to separate out the bits of seaweed, old rope, and plastic bottles, and count the fish. Then we've got to decide how to sort them out. Then we sort them out.

By my reckoning there are eleven. Eleven concepts of truth; eleven ways of viewing truth; or perhaps eleven aspects or elements of truth. They were: the Hebrew dynamic concept; the 'liveable and fruitful' concept; agreement; self-evidence; undoubtability; supported by evidence; direct experience; relationships; love; the will; and rightness and goodness.

Now we've got a problem. Here we are, surrounded with all sorts of ideas and aspects that could possibly go to make up truth. Some may be good, and some may be bad. Some we want to keep, some we want to throw away. Some we want to stress as foundational; some we are willing to accept as contributory. But how do we decide which is which? What's the principle by which we decide this fish should be thrown away, and that one fried for dinner? Presumably because we know that one is edible, and the other isn't. 'Is it edible?' is the test. That works for fish; but what test are we to have for truth? And how do we know that we've got the right test? How do we know our test is true? We are trying to find truth, so it doesn't seem very justifiable to assume that some test is true before we've even decided what truth is. But we can't decide what truth is until we've got a test to help us decide. We're back at the slippery slope argument we looked at towards the end of chapter six. To establish a particular view of truth we have to produce arguments that justify adopting it; but then we have to justify the arguments with a fresh set of arguments; and the fresh set of arguments have to be justified by another set of arguments. And so on, for ever. As we saw there, this is a road that none of us can in fact take.

So what do we do? Go back one chapter further. In chapter five, we acknowledged that the odds are stacked in favour of the sceptics; it is much easier to demolish than build. Constructing a set of beliefs, even about the nature of truth itself, is not the soft option. But we claimed there that, though we may never do it perfectly, we can and should at least have a go. We may not get it right first time, and if we don't we can have another try. But, in an area of life on which so much depends, it hardly seems right to give up before we even begin.

So, in this matter of deciding what test we will use to help find the nature of truth, let's try following the procedure we outlined in chapter five. You will remember that instead of starting with certainty, we suggested we start with a theory, a hypothesis, the best and most likely one we can think of. We take this as our working basis to which we are reasonably committed – willing to do some work on showing that we are justified in adopting it, but not so strongly committed to it that we refuse to abandon it if it becomes clear that we've got it wrong. Then we work out and test the implications and applications of this theory, weighing the evidence that appears to confirm it against the evidence that appears to contradict it. Very likely, as we test it, the longer it survives, the stronger it will get, though it will never reach the point where we can claim to have proved it in the logically watertight or mathematical theorem way. Should we reach the point where the counter-evidence clearly outweighs the positive evidence, then we will have to adjust or abandon the theory and start again.

So there is an element of risk. Right from the start – the basis for our foundational concept of truth, and what we allow into it and what we reject – we're not dealing with something that is totally logically proved. We may not get it right; we may get it partly right and have to adjust it later on; but at least we are going to try something, and do all we can to get it as near to right as possible.

* * *

Consistency and comprehensiveness

So, we take a deep breath and think of the best and most likely test for deciding which elements to include in our concept of truth. For me it can be summed up in two words: consistency and comprehensiveness. Our test to decide which fish to keep is edibility: is it good to eat? To decide which elements I want to include in my concept of truth I ask of each 'Is it consistent? Does it fit? Is the result comprehensive? Does it cover everything that needs to be covered?'

Consistency needs a bit more definition. Consistent with what? Just about everything. With life; with my experience; with other people's experience; with the world around us; with our 'inner' world of consciousness and thought and feeling; with itself; with other elements that go to make up truth; with anything that we believe is real. The more things it is consistent with, and the better everything fits together, the more sure I shall be that I've got it right. The more oddities or unexplained and unexplainable elements of life and experience – the less happy I will be.

It may well be that a test of consistency and comprehensiveness will let in a lot. I'm happy with that. I have a gut feeling that truth is big; there is lots of it, and it applies in lots of areas. We've already seen that there is a very close link between truth and knowledge and communication and meaning; it seems to me that there is a huge number of things to know, and that we can know them in a number of ways; we are all aware that there is a vast amount of communication already going on, and there seems to be no limit to what we can learn from others, or what we can communicate to them; and there is still plenty of meaning to be discovered and explored and understood. Further, the world is big and complex, and the human heart and mind have a lot to them. For too long the tendency has been to try and reduce human persons to animals or machines; but there is much more to us than there is to animals and machines. Maybe we need to be stretched a bit, instead of being reduced.

So, given this test, let's do the opposite of what many have done when they have defined truth in a narrow and limited way. Let's go for a very broad concept of truth, willing to bring in all the elements we've looked at in the last two chapters, excluding only any that don't stand up to the test of consistency and comprehensiveness.

★ ★ ★

Testing the concept   161

A test is a test, so we may as well set our test out in the form of an exam paper. But we'll make it the kind of exam we all dream about: one with the answers included. At least, they'll be my answers. You may well want to check on them and improve them where necessary.

The first couple of questions maybe need a bit of explaining. Of the eleven possible elements we looked at in chapters eight and nine, the first two were pretty practical: the Hebrew dynamic concept, and Mary's 'live-able and fruitful' concept. The next four were broadly rational: agreement, self-evidence, undoubtability, and supported by evidence. The other five were rather more personal: direct experience, relationships, love, the will, and rightness and goodness. Although the focus in our culture has been almost exclusively on the rational aspects, this balance between practical, rational and personal seems a healthy one; it certainly makes for comprehensiveness, and we might feel it is particularly suitable to give a rich and broad concept of what truth is.

But, of course, we need immediately to test this linking up of the three areas of the practical, the rational and the personal by our test of consistency: can the three be held together? Are they consistent with each other and with the way we find things are in the world? Or do we have to follow the trend which tells us to put them into isolated compartments? Or, to put the question another way round: do we as persons do things and reason in an integrated way, or are we conscious that our reasoning is isolated from our personhood, and our doing things is isolated from the other two?

There is a second general area where we need to apply our test of consistency. We're contemplating including no less that eleven ideas or aspects in our view of truth. Is this consistent with our experience? Again, we could rephrase the question: do we find that the nature of truth is something simple and clear and straightforward? Or does it seem by its very nature something complex, many-faceted, involving a number of different aspects?

* * *

JOINT EXAMINING BOARD

Time allowed: as much as you need.
All questions must be attempted.

Question 1 *Does the linking of practical, rational, and personal elements in our concept of truth pass the test of consistency and comprehensiveness?*

It seems to pass the test of comprehensiveness very well, giving us a broad and rich concept of what truth is. It also appears to be fully consistent with our experience. We do things, and we reason, and we are involved in all the range of what being a person means, without splitting ourselves up into watertight compartments. Despite all the philosophers have tried to tell us, each one of us is an integrated whole, not a collection of independent parts. The tendency to divide us up into mind and matter, soul and body, reason and will and emotions, and so on, has been the result of thinkers trying to analyse how we function; but it is not our experience of how we function. We don't in fact differentiate between these various parts of us, nor are we conscious that we are crossing any radical barriers when we appear to switch from one to the other, from, say, thinking to feeling.

163

Question 2 *Does the suggestion that truth may be complex and many-faceted fit the test of consistency and comprehensiveness?*

Again, it helps a lot towards comprehensiveness. And it is certainly consistent with our experience that truth is complex and many-faceted. It seems unlikely that thinkers would have spent so much time debating the nature of truth, some reaching such sceptical conclusions, and some presenting so many different ideas and explanations, if truth was something simple and straightforward. Truth, as a key part of a very complex world, appears itself to be pretty complex.

Question 3 *Assess the concept that undoubtability and self-evidence are key elements of truth.*

We weren't very impressed with the concept of undoubtability when we looked at it in chapter eight; lots of true things can and have been doubted. Additionally, we didn't like the thought of the basis for truth being located in our psychological state. 'I'm sure I put the keys in my pocket' is a claim to be without doubt, but it doesn't give us any truth about where we might find the missing keys.

If we apply our test of consistency, it seems clear we should reject undoubtability as a basic element of truth. It would be quite inconsistent with the way we actually operate in the real world to demand that a thing be undoubtable before we accept it as true. In real life we accept plenty of things that are not beyond doubt as true; and, as a rule, when we do so, instead of causing chaos, everything works out fine. If we are going to be consistent with the way the world actually is, and the way we operate in the world, we cannot demand undoubtability as a basis for truth.

As for comprehensiveness, this suggestion of undoubtability seems to be trying to narrow down the field of truth rather than helping to expand it to cover the whole range of possibilities. The most we can say is that a comprehensive view of truth will need to include the existence of some undoubtable truths.

Much the same applies to self-evidence. To demand that everything we call truth should be self-evidently true seems quite out of keeping with the way we actually operate. We accept all sorts of things as true without demanding that they be self-evident to us or to anyone. If we are going to be consistent with the way we and the world around us generally function, we can't make self-evidence basic to truth. As for comprehensiveness, the same applies as we said for undoubtability; the most we can say is that a comprehensive concept of truth will allow for the existence of some self-evident truths.

Question 4 *Can truth be linked with agreement?*

This brings us to the gawky starlings: if everyone agrees starlings are gawky, then starlings are gawky. It didn't take us long in chapter eight to spot the snags with this, including the fact that total agreement that the earth was flat never managed to stop it being spherical. If we again ask: 'Is the concept that truth is based on agreement consistent with the way we generally operate in the everyday world?', we can safely answer No. We don't feel that that we have to get full agreement before we claim something is true; it is quite consistent for us to say 'I know you don't agree, but Edinburgh really is further west than Cardiff'.

But there is an interesting point here. Although agreement certainly can't be the basis for truth, if we are to be consistent with the way we actually do things, we are going to have to say that the agreement or disagreement of others does have some effect on what we hold to be true. It can't be the deciding factor, but it can be a supporting or subsidiary factor. As we saw in chapter five, if a lot of people agree with what we, on other grounds, have accepted to be the truth, this helps to confirm it for us; while the fact that a lot of people disagree should cause us to have second thoughts, and check out the grounds for their disagreement, in case we have got it wrong.

Certainly, the element of the agreement of others is a significant one when we apply the test of comprehensiveness. In marked contrast to the kind of view that pictures us each looking at the world through our own unique pair of spectacles, each seeing something different and finding only truth-for-me, there is tremendous strength in the confirmation we get from discovering that others see and experience things the same way as we do. Instead of millions of individual ways of seeing things, we find one comprehensive way. I see a tree; the person next to me sees the same tree; and the next person; and the next . . . . Further, in cases where we disagree, if we then talk together and learn from each other and adjust our view to accommodate the new insights we get from others, we feel we are likely to have arrived at a more comprehensive truth.

Question 5 *The fourth of our broadly rational keys to the nature of truth was the existence of adequate evidence. How does this one stand up to the test of consistency and comprehensiveness?*

Unlike the three we've looked at so far, this one certainly does seem to be consistent with the way people do arrive at what they claim to be true. Clearly, supporting evidence is of crucial importance in scientific investigations and criminal trials; the evidence of the atlas settles the issue of Cardiff and Edinburgh; the evidence of five years' residence at Bridlington convinces us that it is on the coast. So we will be very consistent with the way we and the world actually function if we claim that the existence of adequate evidence is a key factor in truth. It may be, incidentally, the reason why the agreement of others is a significant factor even if it is not a key element of truth, as we have just been seeing; in many cases the fact that others have examined the evidence and come to the same conclusions as us is itself an additional piece of supporting evidence.

Evidence also sits happily with our test of comprehensiveness; the more wide-ranging the evidence, and the more thoroughly we examine it, and the more it is confirmed by others, the stronger our conviction that we have found the truth.

167

Question 6 *Moving from the broadly rational to the more personal ways of understanding what truth is, what role should we give to personal experience?*

There doesn't seem much doubt that this one will pass our tests of consistency and comprehensiveness. We've already said that for most people personal experience is a major source of truth: 'I saw it with my own eyes', 'I was there when it happened', and so on. It certainly is consistent with the way we actually function in the world. Additionally, when we were looking at the issue of personal experience in the last chapter, we noticed that one reason we put high truth value on personal experience is because the things we experience are themselves consistent; our experiences fit together and make sense. As for comprehensiveness, one of the things we have to ask of a theory of truth is that it should be wide enough to cover all the rich variety of our, and everyone's, personal experience, from seeing trees to feeling pain.

Question 7 *And what about the element of relating?*

This one doesn't seem quite so straightforward. You will remember that this was the element that went a stage beyond experiencing; we said it is possible simply to experience something and remain unaffected; alternatively, we can be affected, be changed, respond in some way, with pleasure, fear, interest, or whatever; instead of being a detached observer, we become involved.

If we had asked the ancient Hebrews whether this concept of relating fitted consistently with their experience of knowing truth, I'm sure they would have said it did. As we saw at the start of chapter eight, truth for them was something to be engaged with and involved in. But our culture sees things rather differently. We tend to take the detached scientific investigator as our model; such a person seeks for truth and deliberately does not get involved; they operate more as a machine than a person, observing, noting, measuring, and so on, but not responding or letting their personal feelings or attitudes be affected in any way.

Of course, in the last two or three decades there has been a swing away from taking the detached scientific observer as our model for discovering and knowing truth. Science itself is now saying that such detachment is impossible, and many people feel that the attitude of cold detachment, however successful it may have been, has in some ways been inadequate and even detrimental, in that it views both us and the world more or less as machines, and misses out on much of the fulness of truth. We might also add that in our personal experience the truths that we do get involved with and react to will appear more real, and even more true, to us because of that.

Even so, faced with the test of consistency with our general experience of knowing truth, I'm not sure that we can claim that this element of relating or being involved is basic; we can't say in our culture that personal involvement is essential to truth. Perhaps the most we can say is that it could well be a subsidiary factor. As for comprehensiveness, we have to say again that though relating may be an aspect of a fully comprehensive view of truth, we certainly would not want to limit truth to what we personally relate to.

Question 8 *And what about love and the will?*

Very much the same applies. We've managed quite satisfactorily for a very long time without including these as essential elements in truth, so we can hardly start claiming now that they are basic. Even so, if we are seeking to form a broad and rich concept of the nature of truth, there seems no reason why we shouldn't have a go at including these elements in some way, on the grounds that these are essential aspects of what it means to be a person, and if we are going to be consistent with our nature as persons we should try and fit them in.

But in one sense when we apply the test of comprehensiveness, these last three fare rather better. The three elements they introduce, relating, love and the will, are all central to human living; take any one of them away and we would be much less human; take all three away and we probably would not be human at all. So any comprehensive theory of truth is going to need to find a significant place for each of these.

Question 9 *Where does rightness and goodness fit in?*

TRUTH: COULD IT BE TRUE?

Question 10 *Assess the concept of truth as something liveable and fruitful, and the closely related Hebrew concept of truth as something to be lived.*

Since the suggestion that truth might be linked with rightness and goodness first came up in our discussion of the concept of truth as liveable and fruitful, we will take these two questions together.

Once again, if we want our concept of truth to be as comprehensive as possible, there seems to be good reason to include these elements in it. After all, they are pretty significant issues, of considerably greater importance than, say, the issues of the undoubtability or self-evidence of truth. Despite the qualms of the philosophers, there does seem to be a close link between truth and rightness and goodness, and the concept of truth that you live as well as believe is a very attractive one.

To accept the concept that there is a practical aspect in truth does not mean we have to adopt the position of Mary Praxis, which we looked at in chapter six and chapter eight. People who hold this position have gone to the extreme of saying that the practical aspect is the only one; truth is to be defined solely in practical terms, such as what we can live with, or what works. We are back again with the tendency to compartmentalize: truth must go in just one slot, the rational, or the personal, or the practical. But why? Can it not span all three? After all, we do; we are rational and practical persons; the compartments are not totally and irreversibly segregated. The tendency to compartmentalize makes it almost inevitable that those who produce theories about the nature of truth will go to extremes. If, for example, we believe that it simply is not possible for truth to be, say, partly rational and partly non-rational, then, when we find some problem with a view of truth that puts it in the rational compartment, we have no choice but to take it out of that compartment altogether, and put it into a completely different one which is totally 171 non-rational. So we get the extreme positions that have been so common in recent years: truth has to be either wholly external or wholly internal, either wholly theoretical or wholly practical, wholly rational or wholly non-rational, and so on.

As far as concerns consistency, the relevance of consistency to liveability is highlighted in the basic question we have been asking all through this chapter: 'Can we live consistently with this way of viewing truth?' It is not all that big a step to move from 'Can I live with this truth?' to 'Can I live this truth?'. We saw towards the end of the last chapter that though linking truth with rightness and goodness is generally out of fashion, the three concepts have a good deal in common; certainly there is no inconsistency between them.

★ ★ ★

The exam is over. How have we done? There were some pretty hard questions there. Have we made it?

You can certainly award yourself a pass, if only for having a good go at questions that professional philosophers find very tricky. Certainly, most of the answers could be improved on, but at the very least, they lay a good foundation for a consistent and comprehensive approach to truth. In the last part of this chapter, we will try and draw some of the ideas together.

Truth . . . personal, rational, practical

Our analysis has led us to three key aspects of truth that would appear to be essential if we are to have a comprehensive theory of the nature of truth that is consistent with the world we live in and the way we find that we function as people. These three aspects are the personal, the rational, and the practical. In accepting the rational as a key aspect, we are agreeing with the traditional Western concept of truth from as far back as the ancient Greeks, though it was a particular and at times exclusive emphasis from the Enlightenment onwards. In placing the practical alongside the rational, we are reintroducing an element that has been largely neglected, though it was central for the ancient Hebrews, and has been making something of a comeback in the past century. In adding the personal aspect to the other two we are counteracting the tendency of the last two or three centuries to split off and largely ignore those elements of human personhood which don't fit neatly into a scientific world view; we want to insist that the things that mark us off as different from a computer or a machine are at least as important as the things we have in common with computers or machines.

As we have gone through our eleven possible elements that go to make up truth, three have stood out, one each from the three general aspects of the personal, the rational and the practical. These we can take as key elements, highlighting the thrust of the three general aspects. They are the elements of direct personal experience, evidence, and living. To put it succinctly, we could say that truth is something we experience, test, and live.

Under the first heading, experience, I would want to add at least some of the subsidiary elements which stress our response to truth. I'm not sure that I'm happy with the concept that truth is simply something that I am confronted with. To picture myself standing in front of a tree and receiving the truth, 'Here is a tree', in a totally passive way does not seem adequate; there must be some response in me, some linking up of the external facts and my internal acknowledging of them. So, to do justice to the basic personal aspect of truth I would like to add the concept of response to that of experience; as we have seen, that response may take the form of relating, love, or the exercise of my will, or maybe some other form.

Under the second heading, evidence, I would want to include the subsidiary point of agreement. One form of evidence, one way we test a claim to truth, is by checking out the experience and beliefs of others.

Perhaps we could picture truth as a circle, illustrating its comprehensiveness. The overall circle is made up of three concentric circles, but the dividing lines between them are very thin, illustrating that the three aspects they picture are to be seen much more as making up an integrated whole than clearly separated off from each other. The innermost circle, where each one of us starts, is the personal, highlighted by the elements of experience and response. The next circle is the rational, highlighted by evidence and, to some extent, agreement; once we have personally experienced a truth and begun to respond to it, our reason gets to work on it, checking that it is adequately supported by evidence, confirming that it really is true. The outer circle is the practical one; truths, as we respond to them and confirm them, are for living, for putting into practice.

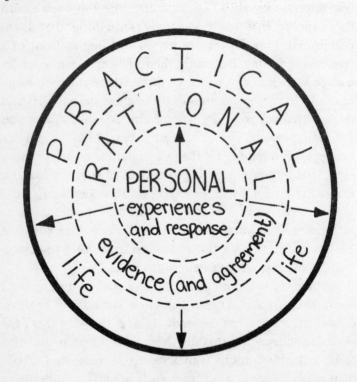

Have we got it right? Is this a full and complete understanding of the nature of truth, the last word to be said on the subject? Assuredly no. But I am quite sure it is a fuller and more correct understanding of truth than its rivals. It is richer and fuller and more true to life than the view that stresses the rational to the exclusion of all other aspects, or the view that defines truth purely in terms of the inward and ignores anything that is external. At the very least it is a good starting point, from which we can begin to go forward. As we do so, we will be able to explore its implications and applications, and put it to the test, and doubtless in due course develop or modify it here and there.

II
Views

At the bottom of the road is a row of shops. Some seem to do a reasonable trade, but for the past few years there have always been some left unoccupied. Times are tough, and competition and rents are high. In the past few years we've lost a DIY shop, a glazier, a greengrocer, an iron-monger, a second-hand dealer, and various others. They come for a time; they struggle; then suddenly they've gone. The place is left empty, desolate, waiting for some-one else to come and try and make a living out of selling flowers, or plumbing, or gearboxes . . . .

Maybe I imagined it, but I was passing by the other day, and saw that one of the empty ones had been re-occupied. The inside had been spruced up, the windows cleaned off, and a large sign-board announced the new business. It simply said *Views*, which wasn't very helpful; so I crossed the road to find out what they were selling – pictures, binoculars, learned magazines, or what.

In the window, elegantly poised on shapely stands, were dozens of pairs of spectacles, or glasses, as I tend to call them. Inside more were on display. I guess the designs of the different pairs varied, but that wasn't the thing that attracted my attention. What caught my eye was their colours. Not the colours of the rims or of the bits that fit behind your ears, but the colour of the glass. Every pair was different: yellow, grey, purple, red, brown, mauve, and so on. All the colours you could think of, the full range.

Somehow I found myself inside the shop. There was no one there, so I had a look around. On the wall there was a display of blue glasses – twenty or thirty of them, all different shades of blue, from navy and midnight blue, through Coeruleum and Corfu blue, to the palest hint of a frosty sky on a winter's morning blue. I rather liked the thought of Corfu, so I tried them on.

My world changed. Everything was blue. Corfu blue. Not that everything was the same; things were still distinct from each other. The bus passing by was a different Corfu blue from the Corfu blue dog walking its Corfu blue owner past the shop. The Corfu blue noses of the people on the bus were all subtly different; but they were all blue. Everything was blue. A strong, bright, clean, Corfu blue. I rather liked it. It was different, and exhilarating. After all, anything that makes Watford feel like Corfu has got to be good.

Then I had a go at the navy blue glasses. Different. Very different. Nothing against the navy, but pretty depressing. Everything, a dark shade of blue. Distinctly gloomy. I took them off and tried the pale blue.

Different again. Crisp, bright, alive. Everything pale blue; not just a pale blue sky, but a pale blue post box being emptied by a pale blue postperson. Delicate blue carrots on display outside the pale blue supermarket being selected by the local vicar in a shimmering silver blue suit. A whole new world of pale blue.

* * *

'Now then, what can I do for you?' asked the man who had come through the door at the back of the shop. 'Which pair is it you want?'

'I don't know,' I replied. 'In fact I'm not at all sure that I want any.'

'But of course you do. Everybody has to choose some

way of viewing things. You can't get by with no glasses at all.'

'Oh, I seem to have managed OK so far without any,' I said.

'Not at all. Look.' He held a mirror up and I saw that what I had always taken as my bushy eyebrows and bags under my eyes were really a pair of glasses, which I must have worn for years without knowing it; they'd been there so long that they'd kind of grown in and become part of me. 'Everyone has glasses. Everyone has to see the world in one way or another. Everybody has a basic world view. Even those who are quite sure they haven't and try to claim they are totally unbiased and see the world exactly as it is. No one can do that. Everyone has glasses.'

'Well, in that case, I can carry on with the pair I've got.'

'You could. But your pair is pretty old. And look at the range I've got here. And some very good bargains. This one, for instance. I'm selling this colour very cheap – it's a discontinued range. We call it Marxist red.'

I didn't like the look of it, and told him so. If I was going to have anything, I'd like something a bit more relevant to today.

'Then you need something in the green line,' he replied. 'very popular at the moment, and a huge range. Are you religious?'

The question caught me off guard, so I muttered something about being that way inclined.

'Green, and pretty religious,' he said, scanning his wares. 'How about this one?'

'This one' was a mellow viridian. I put it on. The world changed. Green. Alive, growing, verdant. I glanced through the window, and saw that the road outside was a meadow, a rich water meadow, with grass and reeds lush in the afternoon sunshine. I'd never seen the trees over by the railway looking so alive, every leaf vibrant with green vitality. And the cabbages outside the supermarket; luscious, juicy, huge; dynamic cabbages; cabbages to end all cabbages. All around me, a living world. Rich with life. And power. Pulsating with power. Power in the earth. Mother earth. Gaia. The source. The womb. Rich and strong and prolific. Teeming with life. And I was part of it. I belonged. I too was alive. Like the grass and the trees and the cabbages and the earth. Together with them. One with them. The life force, the divine, Spirit − and me. It was powerful, heady, intoxicating. Everything fitted into place. The world, life, nature, God, me, the cabbages. My blood throbbed; I wanted to dance, in tune with the song of earth, beating out the rhythm of some pagan ritual. . .

'You like them?' said a voice, and there was the shopkeeper standing at my side.

'No, I'm not sure that I do,' I replied. 'They're a bit on the strong side for me.'

'But they're good. Very good. Lots of people are going for them.'

'Yes, I can see they give you an interesting point of view.'

'Oh, not just interesting. Very full, very rich. They give you a place in the world. They link you up with divine power. They give you a vision and a purpose. Ecology and peace and religion all rolled into one. Very attractive.'

'Even so, I think I'd like something rather different.'

'Different? Hm. Well, I don't suppose you could get anything much more different than these.' He took a pair from his yellow range, polished them up with a cloth, and gave them to me to put on.

The effect was dramatic. Even though I'd taken off the 183 green glasses, my world still hadn't quite got back to normal; it was still pulsating, alive, growing, though at a slower rate. Now it stopped. Totally. No life. No power. No growth. Inert. Torpid. Dead. Not that there was no movement. A car went past the shop; it was in motion, but not with the movement of life. It moved because the wheels engaged with the road, and the transmission with the wheels, and the gearbox with the transmission, and the engine with the gearbox. Pistons, physical laws, chemical reaction. A machine.

The vicar came out of the supermarket with his bag of carrots. He too was a machine. He moved much the same way as the car moved. His feet moved because his muscles moved; his muscles moved because impulses ran down his nerves. The impulses came from the chemistry of his brain. The vicar was physics and chemistry. He wasn't a soul. He wasn't even a person. Just another machine. The world was a machine. No mother earth. A great lump of matter. Everything according to the laws of science. No freedom; no persons; just a machine. And life was a machine. No pulsating life force or divine creativity. Chemistry again. This chemical and that chemical coming together by chance in a primeval soup. No meaning; no purpose. All in terms of laws of science. All a machine.

'No,' I said, as I took them off. 'No, I want something with more faith in it. We can't just operate like machines. We must have some faith.'

'But this is a faith,' he responded, obviously rather hurt. 'It is as much a faith as any of my glasses. Those who wear these yellow glasses – and they are still the official uniform of our current scientific culture – exercise as much faith in their basic world view as any of the great religions. Though I must admit sales have been going down lately. But there are still plenty of pairs around that people have been wearing for decades; they wear very well, you see. But perhaps you mean you want something more religious?'

'Well, what can you offer me?'

He thought for a moment or two. Then he chose a brown pair. 'Interesting ones, these,' he said. 'They come from Papua New Guinea. I didn't think they'd sell in this country; but they're going quite well. Not vast numbers, but a steady flow.'

By now I was beginning to get the hang of things, so I had an idea of what to expect. Something like the green pair, perhaps, but with more Stone Age flavour. What I got was frightening. Everything was alive again, but with a different sort of life. Not the integrated pulsating life of the green pair, beating out the rhythm of the song of the earth. But spirits. Spirits in the trees. Spirits in the wind. Spirits in the people. The woman with a shopping trolley, driven by malignant spirits. The brown of the glasses made her look unreal; her shopping trolley was unreal; but the spirits weren't unreal. They were real, all right; much too real. They made her walk. They made her glance quickly at us in the shop and then hurry on. They made the van drive past. One day they would make the van drive into her and over her and crush the life from her body.

I pulled the glasses off. 'For goodness' sake,' I said, 'Give me something better than that; haven't you got anything Christian?'

'Yes, of course. This is the Christian section over here. Quite a variety. What brand of Christianity would you like?'

I looked at the display. There certainly was a variety. Quite a few dull musty looking greys. A pair that looked like stark black and white. And a lively, trendy looking section.

'I've a feeling these would be just about right for you. A very fine pair of glasses indeed. A bit on the dear side, but well worth it.'

He was right. Not too trendy, but certainly not musty. I put them on, and drew a deep breath.

The world was alive again. Not with the terrifying confusion of spirits. Nor with the intoxicating dance of mother earth. But with meaning and purpose. Not chance, not an impersonal process. But everything created, made for a purpose, a good purpose. Truth and harmony. Love; yes, that was what it was; the place was alive with love. It had all been lovingly planned and put together, and someone was at this moment pouring out love on it all. A good love. Not a selfish lustful love. But wholesome and pure. Love and goodness. Like light being poured out on everything – the cyclist propping her bike against the kerb; the dog waiting outside the supermarket, the flowers in the hanging baskets outside the hair-dresser's.

Not everything reacted the same way to the love and the goodness. Some – the flowers and the cyclist – received it and absorbed it and were made more real and whole by it; they seemed themselves to radiate it. Others – the racist graffiti on the supermarket wall and the video posters in 'Hollywood Nites' – seemed to fling it back with contempt and hatred. But still it came, strong and beautiful. For a moment I seemed to catch its vision of a world without evil and hatred and violence and sin; a broken world restored; a groaning, hurting world made whole.

I didn't see where the love was coming from. But I knew. Not from the earth itself, but from the one who planned and made and loves the earth. A personal creator God. Full of love. Full of goodness. And personal. A person, not a thing. Personal, like me and the man in the shop and the people at the bus stop. Or rather, we are personal like him. He is real personhood; he made us with bits in us that are like him, so that we could love and radiate goodness and share our lives with others and with him.

And at that point he came. He was in the shop. His love was being poured over me. I wanted to fall to the floor. I wanted to shout. The living God. The one who comes. Holy and mighty and full of grace and truth.

★ ★ ★

When I eventually took the glasses off, the man was sitting

reading his newspaper. 'You want those?' he said. 'They'll set you back a bit.'

'Yes,' I said. 'I want those. I don't mind what they cost.'

At that moment Nicky came into the shop. She's a neighbour of mine, and was soon pretty interested in the display of glasses.

'So you can choose any pair you like?' she said. 'Off the hook world views. You pays your money and you takes your choice.' She wandered round the shop, studying the range. 'So I can choose any pair at all?'

'Yes,' said the man. 'Any pair at all. And I've lots more out the back.'

'So it's a kind of blind leap of faith. All these different world views, and I can just adopt any one of them. Anyone can choose to believe what they like, put on any pair of glasses; and that decides how they see the world. You adopt a world view just by faith, for no reason at all.'

'Some do,' said the man. 'Some just grab the first pair they see, and don't ask any questions. But others are very choosey; they try a lot on before they decide. This gentleman here, for instance, tried several different pairs.'

'Then what made you select that pair?' Nicky asked me. 'Why did you reject the others?'

'Well, it certainly wasn't a blind leap of faith,' I replied. 'I had good reasons for choosing as I did. They were all interesting, and most of them had good points and bad points. But the pair I chose seem to fit best overall; they gave the best explanation of the whole of life and the

whole of the universe – physical, moral, personal, spiritual, practical – the lot.'

'But how do you know it is right? Have you been able
to prove that it's true?'

'Well, proving its truth takes time. It's a process, rather
than something you can do all at once and for ever. You
test it out; you live it; you check it with reality. And
hopefully, it gets more and more confirmed as you go
on.'

'But suppose I choose these,' she said, picking up the
Marxist red pair that were still lying on the table. 'You
have your Christian view; I have my Marxist view. Who's
to say which is right? According to my Marxist principles,
your Christianity is rubbish. According to your Christian
principles my Marxism is rubbish. How can we decide
which world view is true? Surely any pair of glasses, any
set of beliefs, is as valid as any other? They all have to be
taken on faith.'

'Well, yes, I accept everyone uses faith to adopt their
world view, even the atheists. But it isn't a blind faith;
most people have reasons for choosing the one they adopt;
they check it out and see if they like the feel of it, see if it
makes sense, and so on. So it's a kind of reasonable faith,
not a blind faith.

'And there's nothing to stop two people with different
world views debating together which one fits all the facts
best, which one is the most true to life, works best, and so
on. There's that process I was saying about; as time goes by
your beliefs get more confirmed because they fit and
work, or get increasingly discredited until you reach the
point where you have to drop them. That's exactly what

happened with Marxism. Lots of people believed in it and tried it out; but for most of them now it has been discredited; it isn't true. The same applies to some versions of Christianity. Lots of people have tried to combine Christianity with the 'Everything is a machine' world view, and produce a kind of watered down version with only a very small role for God. It might look OK in theory, but as time has gone by people have found it just doesn't work. That kind of Christianity's being abandoned all over the place.'

'Hang on a moment,' said Nicky. 'Are you trying to say that you can in the end show that your Christianity is true and that every other world view is false?'

'Well, not really. I'm certainly not saying that every other world view is false if by false you mean totally mistaken. There's a huge amount of overlap. I can quite happily say that the vast majority of what a Marxist or an atheist believes is true. We all agree that Edinburgh is north of London, that water boils at 100°, and so on. It's the same with other religions; there's a terrific amount of truth in them. But if an atheist says there is no God, and a Hindu says there are lots of Gods and I say there is one God, provided we are all using the word "God" in the same sense, we can't all three be right. So I suppose I'm saying that every world view has lots of truth, but Christianity as a world view is the most consistent and comprehensive and so has the most truth.

'But I don't claim that I can totally prove this to everyone here and now. I've proved it to myself to my own satisfaction, and, as time goes by, my conviction that it is the truth gets stronger. And I'll certainly do what I can

189

to help others find its truth for themselves. But it isn't a matter of producing arguments that force them to become Christians. That isn't the way it is, and I don't think I'd like it if it was. No one should be forced to believe any world view; we all have a free choice.'

'So you don't want to go around forbidding people from disagreeing with you. You're quite happy for this shop to open up here?'

'I'm perfectly happy for people to try out as many world views as they like, and see which one is the most consistent and comprehensive. Of course, I hope that they don't ignore Christianity; since I believe that is the true one, I'm naturally keen that they each give it a go. That's why I'm into the business of telling people what the basic beliefs of Christianity are; lots of people reject it without giving it a fair try.'

'And what about faith? Did I hear you say that all world views need at least some faith?'

'Yes, I think they do,' I replied. 'But I tried to say it shouldn't be blind faith; we need to be able to justify why we put our faith in this set of beliefs rather than that set.'

'But isn't religious faith very different from, say, the faith the scientists have in their world view?'

'It is different in some ways, but I don't think it is radically different. Suppose an atheist scientist says, "I believe everything happens strictly according to the laws of physics." He can't prove that; it is an article of faith; though no doubt he could produce good reasons why he believes it. Then a Christian says, "I believe most things happen according to the laws of physics, but sometimes God steps in and does something outside the laws of physics, like the creation or a miracle." Now she can't prove that, either; it is an article of faith. But I don't think the beliefs are radically different sorts of beliefs, or that the kinds of faith the two of them are exercising are very different.'

'But isn't there more commitment in religious faith?'

'I think there probably ought to be, but often there isn't. Lots of Marxists have been far more committed to their world view than many Christians to theirs. I happen to believe that the Christian way of life taught us by Jesus does call for quite a bit of commitment, but, again, I wouldn't say it is anything radically different from being committed, say, to a political party or to a "green" lifestyle. I think there certainly are elements of Christianity that are very distinctive – its stress on a personal God we can know, and the centrality of love, for example. So when we are talking of faith and commitment in the context of our relationship to a God of love we are obviously talking of something very different from faith or commitment to a set of ideas. But that is because God is so very different from a set of ideas.'

★ ★ ★

Time was going. I had things to do. I paid for my glasses, left Nicky to choose hers, and walked out into the street.

12
Argument

As I drove round a gentle right-hand bend on a wide piece of road, a white van coming in the opposite direction headed straight for me. For a moment the driver seemed to be regaining control, and I thought he might miss me. But, no; he smashed into me, mercifully on the side rather than the front, swung me round and up onto the verge, while he ended up on the grass bank some distance further down the road.

Months later I was still trying to get some money out of my insurers. Clearly, there was a conflict of interests between them and me: my interest was to get the money and theirs was to avoid paying. One approach they tried was insisting the car was a three-door model, which was valued at several hundred pounds less than the five-door model. I had owned the car, had opened and closed all five doors many times, and was quite convinced it was a five-door model. They, equally, according to their letters, were convinced it was a three-door model.

There are plenty of people who would argue that Highway Motor Policies at Lloyds were as right in saying that it was a three-door model as I was in saying it was a five-door model. You will have gathered from what I've written in this book that I didn't take that view. I was certain it was a five-door model. I wasn't prepared to accept that its five-doorness was a truth for me, but not for them. For me it was a universal truth, a truth that they should recognize as much as I did.

So here was an argument in the area of truth. That is the theme of this chapter. Whatever people may say, conflicts and arguments do arise in the real world, and, mercifully, there are various ways in which we can seek to resolve them.

Not that I'm saying that every conceivable conflict that might arise has to be argued out and resolved. Life is too short for that. Had Highway Motor Policies tried insisting that the car was a particularly unpleasant colour, or that it wasn't the wisest make to buy in the first place, I would have been quite prepared to allow that they were as entitled to their opinion as I was to mine. But when they called the recorded mileage 'unbelievably low' or insisted the car had only three doors, I felt justified in insisting on the truth. Many issues are not worth arguing over; we can accept a diversity of beliefs. But some are. What is it that makes the difference?

* * *

Significant issues

Some would suggest the difference is to do with the distinction between scientific truth and other sorts of belief, or between facts and values. Scientific truth or facts, like water boiling at 100° or Edinburgh being north of London, are universal fixed truths, and we are justified in insisting on them; indeed, it would be irresponsible if we didn't. But non-scientific beliefs or values, like 'This car is an unpleasant colour' or 'This make is a bad buy' are not universal; they are personal; we are each entitled to adopt our own beliefs and attitudes in these areas, and to allow others to adopt theirs. None of us has any right to insist that anyone else adopts ours.

For me this approach is too simplistic. I don't think it is possible to make a clear distinction between 'scientific' truth and other beliefs, or between fact and value. If I tried hard enough, I guess I could produce a 'scientific' basis for the 'value' statements: 'This make is a bad buy', and 'This car is an unpleasant colour.' Maybe statistical analysis of performance, depreciation, rust, accident re-cord, and so on would do for the first; and a scientific analysis of what happens to my blood pressure or stomach muscles when I'm confronted with that colour would do for the second. Even if my value statement was pure prejudice, like 'Drivers of red cars are more dangerous than other drivers', it would still be possible to find a 'scientific' explanation for my prejudice; I might, for example have been knocked out of my push chair by a red car when I was a baby. Once again, I'm not at all convinced that we should divide our world and truth up into segregated compartments.

Additionally, at any rate in our current culture, we do in practice see certain value statements as universal truths and insist on everyone accepting them, for example: 'Men and women are of equal value'.

So my way of telling which issues are worth arguing for and which are not is not going to depend on any distinction between scientific fact and 'value'; rather, I would want to ask what difference holding or rejecting this or that belief will make. Will it have a significant effect on our lives or on the lives of others? If so, it is something worth taking trouble to establish one way or the other. The distinction between a three-door car and a five-door car had considerable financial implications, so it was worth arguing for; what Highway Motor Policies felt about the colour meant nothing to me and little to them, so I would have been happy to let it go. Similarly, prejudice against either men or women can have far-reaching effects, so the issue of what value we put on each of the sexes is worth arguing for.

A very important point arises from this. At any given time we can judge that an issue is of very small practical importance; it will have little or no effect on other people's lives, so we can accept that it is not worth making a fuss about. But it is always conceivable that what is insignificant today may become very significant some time in the future. Take, for example, this issue: 'Edinburgh has a more pleasant climate than London.' Most of us would readily accept that this is largely a matter of personal opinion, and not the kind of issue whose truth we would bother to try and establish one way or the other. 'You believe Edinburgh's more pleasant and I believe London's more pleasant; each of us is entitled to our opinion.' But suppose the organizers had come down to a short list of two for the location for the next World Trade Fair, and those two were London and Edinburgh; in all other respects the two cities were equally suitable, and the clinching factor turned out to be which had the more pleasant climate; that would then become a very significant issue, one well worth working hard on and arguing to establish.

I would suggest, then, that there are some issues where it is important to establish and agree the truth. These are issues that will have a significant effect on people's lives, like whether or not planes for Edinburgh should land ten minutes north of London, or whether the car is a three-door or five-door model. There are other issues where deciding one way or the other will make little or no difference to people's lives, such as 'That car is an unpleasant colour', or 'The shape of that cloud reminds me of Uncle Jack.' Here there seems little or no need to establish the truth; most of us would be happy to allow that in this kind of area if someone disagrees with us they have a right to their opinion and we are not going to argue with them. However, it is always conceivable that something we feel is an unimportant issue today may at some time in the future become an important issue worth arguing over.

* * *

The purpose of argument and basic beliefs

What are we seeking to do when we engage in argument? We might be tempted to reply 'Win'; and that may seem to be a perfectly adequate answer for those who reject any concept of fixed truth. But for me the right answer is 'To establish the truth'; though we enter the argument convinced that our view is the right one, we have seen that we must never be so committed to our position that we refuse to allow the possibility that we may be wrong; arguing must involve listening to the other side just as much as stating our own. So arguing should be a dialogue, stating and listening to the case for each side, and the evidence that supports each case, until both sides can reach agreement over what they can accept as the truth.

In many cases, conflict arises simply from lack of adequate information or communication. No one in the claims department which insisted my car had three doors had ever set eyes on it, nor did they show any interest in travelling to Bedford to check it for themselves. Yet the information was available, and the argument could easily have been resolved. So the primary task of those whose beliefs conflict is to get together as many as possible of the facts of the case and the supporting evidence. This can take all sorts of forms: on the ground investigation, consulting an accepted authority, weighing up evidence, analysing counter-evidence, and so on.

In some cases, however, things are not so easy. The evidence is there, and both sides accept it, but it is open to more than one interpretation. As we have seen, we all inevitably approach the evidence with a certain degree of bias; we interpret what we see according to our basic set of beliefs. It is just conceivable that the man from the claims department might be so convinced that I was trying to pull a fast one on them, that even if he and I stood together in front of the five-door car in the salvage company's yard in Bedford, he still would not admit defeat: 'What you've done is taken the number plates off your three-door car and stuck them on this five-door wreck.'

If that happens I could continue trying to find evidence that would convince him, like producing photographs, or a letter from the manufacturer stating that the car with the given chassis and engine numbers was a five-door model (the course I actually took); or I could accept that whatever evidence I produced he would explain away in acccordance with his conviction that I was a budding fraudster; in that case I would have to move the argument away from the car to my character; if he was going to interpret all the evidence in accordance with his basic belief that I was a fraudster, then that was the issue we needed to sort out; his basic belief had to be changed; I had to persaude him that I was an upright and honest citizen who would never dream of making a fraudulent claim. So instead of a letter from the manufacturers of the car, I needed testimonials from trustworthy people who knew me well.

So there are two possibilities. In most situations we will find that the person we are arguing with agrees with our basic principles ('The number of doors can be settled by seeing the car or by getting a letter from the manufacturer'). But when our basic principles differ, then the level of the argument has to shift, and we have to tackle the question, 'Which set of basic principles is right?' This kind of situation can arise anywhere, and not just in areas like politics and religion. It happens frequently, for example, in science, where the data is interpreted differently by different scientists according to their differing basic theories.

If it were the case, of course, that people adopt basic beliefs or principles purely at random, with no justification at all, it would be very difficult to persuade them by argument to change them. They would always be able to say, 'You have demonstrated clearly that my basic beliefs are false (or unliveable or inconsistent), but I'm still going to believe them'. But in fact we rarely, if ever, adopt basic beliefs entirely at random; there are always some reasons, rational or not so rational, why we adopted them in the first place and why we continue to hold them; and most of us, if we were to be shown that there are good reasons why we should stop holding a particular belief, would be willing to let it go.

I have said that we may have 'not so rational' reasons for adopting or holding a basic belief. By this I certainly don't mean 'irrational'. An irrational belief would be one that we hold contrary to reason, like insisting on three doors when conclusive evidence has proved five doors. A not so rational belief is one we've adopted without thinking it through, balancing up the evidence, and so on. Many of the beliefs we adopt in childhood are of this nature, and even some we adopt as adults: we believe in Father Christmas because mummy tells us about him, or we support a political party because the leader looks good on television. Again, if such beliefs have little or no effect on the way we live, we may get away without ever thinking seriously about them, but sooner or later most such beliefs will need to be checked and tested; and if evidence begins to build up against them, we must be prepared to let them go. We notice that the large gentleman pictured on the Christmas cards could never fit into our chimney, let alone the bike he is supposed to have brought with him; we check out the policies of the particular party and find they are full of inconsistencies. To continue to insist on these beliefs in the face of the evidence would be irrational.

So, if we are arguing on the level of basic principles or underlying beliefs, our task is to seek to analyse the adequacy of those principles. We might be able to point out, for instance, some flaws in their consistency or comprehensiveness which make them less than adequate. Or we might be able to show that the evidence supporting them is poor, or the counter-evidence is strong, while the evidence for an alternative set of basic beliefs is much stronger.

203

* * *

Arguing about religion

Those who say that it is possible to establish truth about scientific facts but not about non-scientific values usually put religion in the second group and conclude that we can never argue for or against the truth of any religion. This ignores not only the fact that arguments and debates for and against the truth of various religions have been going on for centuries, but also that there is a steady stream of people adopting or abandoning this or that religion precisely because they have become convinced that it is true or false. I have talked to many people who have adopted the basic beliefs of Christianity because they have checked out the evidence for their truth and have been convinced by the arguments. Equally, I have talked to those who once believed, but who have passed through some particularly painful experience which has led them to argue that since a God of love would have prevented such an experience, such a God cannot exist.

True, many people adopt religious beliefs for reasons that are less than fully rational. As small children they believe what mummy tells them, or they unthinkingly adopt the ideas of their surrounding culture, or they have a dramatic conversion experience. But, particularly in today's climate, it won't be long before such beliefs are challenged, and are either given a firmer basis through being confirmed by evidence and life, or abandoned as unjustified.

Underlying the approach of those who insist that issues of truth and falsehood do not arise with religious beliefs is the foundational mistake of assuming that religion applies only to a very limited part of us, our religious or spiritual part, and this has nothing to do with the rest of us or the rest of life. So, we are told, religious beliefs or statements can never say anything about the real world: if we say, 'Jesus rose from the dead', we may be expressing some sort of spiritual feeling about life, but we are not claiming anything about an event in the real world some two thousand years ago.

Again, this is quite contrary to the way things actually are. Christianity in particular, but other religions as well, insist that the truths they hold are relevant for the whole of life, and apply across every area. The statement, 'Jesus rose from the dead', is a statement about a real event in the real world, just as much as 'The Tories won the election.' Granted, it has religious or spiritual implications, just as the Tories winning the election has political and social implications, but this does not take away the factual or even 'scientific' truth of the basic statement. Indeed, the apostle Paul goes so far as to say that if the event of the resurrection is not factually true, there can be no spiritual implications: 'If Christ has not been raised, your faith is futile'; the validity of the 'spiritual' faith is bound up with the truth of the real event in the world.

It is worth remembering that, so far from being concerned with just the limited 'spiritual' area of our lives, Christianity's concern and relevance covers every aspect. Because of its clear emphasis on a personal and holy God who creates and upholds and loves everything that exists, it is able to hold closely together the created ('scientific') 205 order with the personal and the spiritual and the emotional and the moral. All of these are built into an integrated whole; there are no divisions into isolated areas; something can be scientifically true and morally true and spiritually true all at the same time. This not only expresses the comprehensiveness of the Christian world view; it gives us the opportunity to reunite the universe and our understanding of it and our living in it, things which have been fragmented by so many recent thinkers.

*   *   *

Truth, dogmatism and tolerance

We have already seen in chapter seven that one of the arguments put forward by those who reject fixed universal truth is that believing in and insisting on finding truth breeds dogmatism and intolerance. Their rejection of the concept of truth means, they claim, that everyone's ideas are equally accepted, and so everyone is equally accepted. All win, and all have prizes.

I have argued that there is such a thing as truth, and though there are very many situations where we most certainly do not need to insist on finding it and getting others to accept it, there are some where we are justified in doing so, and, indeed, could be acting irresponsibly if we do not do so. These are, of course, the kind of situation where establishing the truth would have a significant effect on people's lives or well-being.

We are only too aware that dogmatism and intolerance have arisen in just about every area of knowledge and belief in the past, and that there is still plenty of them around, not least in some religions. But do we have to abandon the concept of truth in order to get rid of them? Is it possible to believe in truth and even argue for it in a way that avoids dogmatism and intolerance, and that accepts all people equally?

I believe it is possible; though I don't think it is easy. The snag is that we are all profoundly influenced by the attitude of our culture, with its concepts of self-assertion and the survival of the fittest, and the belief that the goal of any argument is to win. The alternative attitude is one that lies at the very heart of Christianity, but which even Christians have sometimes failed to practise. It is based on self-denial and humility, and believes that the goal of any argument is the well-being of the other person. One way of expressing it is to take three well-known New Testament phrases which couple other concepts closely with truth:

the truth will set you free
full of grace and truth
speaking the truth in love.

If we could shape our attitude to truth and our approach to discovering and sharing truth around these three concepts of freedom, grace and love, we would, I fancy, avoid the mistakes of dogmatism and intolerance. Our goal would be to set people free, rather than make them slaves of concepts and doctrines and systems. Our approach would be one of grace: instead of judging and condemning others for their views, we would accept and welcome and honour them, as the father did the prodigal son; there is no more contradiction in our giving full acceptance to someone while disagreeing with some of their beliefs than there was in the father welcoming home the boy who had made a mess of just about everything. And the whole thing would be immersed in love: our concern to find and share the truth would be subject to our God-inspired commitment to their wholeness and well-being; people matter more than truth.

Maybe that last phrase isn't quite right. If we take 'truth' to mean no more than my way of seeing things, or logically demonstrated proof, or factual correctness, or pragmatic convenience, or the like, it will of course stand. But the argument of this book is that truth is something much bigger and richer than any of those concepts. It is something that covers the personal as well as the rational and the practical; it is linked with goodness and rightness and wholeness and love; in our final chapter we will be seeing that it is integral to the being of God and inseparable from his holiness and love and life.

So, in a sense, we are saying that truth is the full expression of what it means to be a person, to be truly human, to live as an individual, and in relationship with the world around us, and in community with others. In that sense it is hardly right to set people over against truth; we are back to 'The truth will set you free.' It is truth that makes us people.

13
Foundations

We started this book with everybody winning a race. Since then we've touched on many of the major issues that arise when we begin to think about truth: conflicting beliefs, certainty, interpretation of data, evidence, fixed and changing truth, external and internal truth, truth and culture, doubt and scepticism, trust, faith, commitment, proof, building a set of beliefs, testing beliefs, concepts of truth, and arguing.

It is time we drew our various discussions together. Perhaps the best way of doing that is to put forward ten theses which, for me at any rate, sum up the main points of our discussion. They won't necessarily be perfect or final, and you will no doubt be able to think of ways of improving them. But at least they will lay a good foundation for truth at a time when we desperately need one.

Thesis 1. *Given the complexity of the world and of the human mind, we can accept that truth itself is something complex.*

Attempts to limit truth to something very simple, like 'Only what we can logically prove is true', have not worked. Truth is something big and rich, and it contains many different elements and aspects. Strict 'Either/or' approaches are too simplistic; instead of saying, 'Truth is either wholly outside of us or wholly inside us', we must be prepared to accept that it can be both – partly outside us and partly inside us.

Thesis 2. *Truth has at least three major aspects which should be seen as merging into one another rather than as three isolated areas: the personal, the rational, and the practical.*

These are, of course, aspects that we find in the world around us and in ourselves. The tendency in the past few centuries has been to pick out just one, the rational, and to claim that truth operates in that area alone. Some contemporary overreaction against this approach has claimed that it operates just in the practical area, or just in the personal area. But a balanced holistic approach would seem to need to recognize that it operates in all three, and that the three are not to be separated off as isolated watertight compartments, but as closely related to each other and merging together to make up an integrated whole.

Thesis 3. *The personal aspect of truth has two elements to it. There is an 'external' element: our awareness of things outside of us with which we are presented in personal experience. And there is an 'internal' element: our interpretation and response.*

For most people direct personal experience is the most convincing way of establishing truth: 'I've been there, so I know'. In direct personal experience we appear to be presented with something totally outside of us; we don't create it or shape it; we simply accept it. But very often (if not always) we add an inner personal element to what is given from outside. We interpret the round shape as a rabbit hole, or the complex shape as Buckingham Palace. Further, when we get away from simple drawings into the complexity of real life situations, we add all sorts of inner personal elements to our response to the external data. We feel, we enjoy, we react, we respond, we exercise our will, and so on.

None of this means that we in any way control or do

away with the external data. But we develop our beliefs about it through a complex process in which we build on the basic data in personal and even creative ways through our interpretation and response. However, there are definite limits to how far we can acceptably do this, and these limits are somehow imposed by the basic data. We can interpret a circle as a drawing of a rabbit hole or a drawing of the sun, but we cannot interpret it as Buckingham Palace.

Thesis 4. *The rational aspect of truth is an important part of our response to the data given in personal experience. Its role is not to create truth, but to test it, and to build individual truths into an overall world view.*

While rejecting the view that the rational aspect of truth is its only aspect, we don't want to go to the contemporary extreme of rejecting reason altogether. It has a crucial part to play, often right at the moment of our interpretation of what we personally experience: 'Hang on, that can't be a blackberry bush; it's the best part of seventy feet tall.' And reason certainly has a part to play in building up our beliefs into a consistent and comprehensive world view. Here evidence plays a major role: we check the things we hold to be true by evidence for and against, willing to adjust or abandon them if we get too much counter-evidence, and accepting them as increasingly confirmed if we get lots of positive evidence.

Thesis 5. *The practical aspect of truth brings it out of the realm of theory into that of life. Truth is for living, not just believing.*

TRUTH: COULD IT BE TRUE?

We need to listen again to the ancient Hebrew concept of truth and some of its modern counterparts: truth is primarily to be lived, not just believed; it is itself alive and dynamic, not static; it is something we relate to; we are affected by it and we affect it; in many cases if we claim to believe a truth but it remains mere theory and doesn't affect our living, then there is a sense in which it is untruth.

Thesis 6. *Within the general personal / rational / practical framework there are many elements that go to make up truth; we should not seek to reduce our concept of truth to just one or two of these elements, but seek for a comprehensive and rich concept, which gives due place to them all.*

Some of these elements, for example being undoubtable or morally right and good, are applicable in just a few situations. Others, like commanding general agreement, cover a much wider range. And some, like being supported by evidence, seem to apply across the board.

Thesis 7. *In order to live as individuals we each have to build up a set of beliefs which we accept as truth; in order to live in community with other individuals, we have to have a common set of beliefs we all accept; without this there can be no communication or meaning.*

Everyone has to have a world view; we cannot live with total anarchy. In order to communicate with and understand each other we have to have at least some beliefs in common. Community is built on truth.

It is easier to doubt than to have faith; yet scepticism is unliveable and faith is essential to any world view. It is easier to demolish than to build a world view; therefore we should exercise a degree of commitment in building our set of beliefs.

Thesis 8. *In building a set of beliefs we start with an unproved theory or hypothesis. Over a period of time we work out the implications and applications of this theory, and test it according to evidence for and against it. In time it will become increasingly confirmed, or will need to be modified or abandoned.*

We have to start by accepting something by faith or on trust, and exercise a degree of commitment to it; but our faith or commitment must not be such that we cling to it against all the evidence. Nor is it by any means 'blind' faith; we don't choose a theory at random. We have reasons (rational or non-rational or both) for deciding that this theory rather than that theory is the one we are going to start with. We choose the pair of spectacles that we feel is most likely to fit; we start wearing them, and, as we do so, start checking out that they do fit.

The testing will not all be in the area of rational evidence. Marie's 'testing' of whether or not her parents love her will largely be personal and emotional, but it is just as valid as a rational argument. One of the main ways we test any theory is whether or not we can live with it or live it.

Thesis 9. *Where there is disagreement over issues which have significant bearing on people's lives, we have a duty to try and establish which of the various views is the truth. This can be done* *by constructive argument, either debating the immediate issues, or on the level of basic beliefs.*

Most people agree over most things. Some things we disagree over have little or no significant effect on people's lives, and there seems no reason why we or anyone should try and make them change their views, even if we disagree with them. But when an issue arises which has significant bearing on our lives or the lives of others, then we are justified in seeking to establish the truth of the matter, and even obliged to do so.

The way we do this is of great importance; though we may be convinced we are right and the other person is wrong, our arguing of our case should be marked with humility, grace, love, and a willingness to change our view if it becomes clear that we are in the wrong.

Arguing or debating the evidence for and against specific beliefs is relatively straightforward. But in situations where the two sides start with radically different basic beliefs, it will often happen that those basic beliefs will determine what counts as evidence or how that evidence is interpreted. In that case, little or no progress will be made debating the immediate issues, and the argument will have to switch to the different level of debating the case for or against those basic beliefs.

Thesis 10. *The trend to limit proof to what can be established in a mathematically or logically watertight way is to be rejected. There are many sorts of proof, and we must select the type that is appropriate to the issues we are dealing with, not try to impose one concept of proof over everything. We can still claim that a* *thing has been shown to be true even if there is a remote possibility that it may one day be shown to be false.*

We can claim that a thing is true even if it is not totally undoubtable or logically proved, or even if it is conceivable we may be wrong in our claim. Indeed, almost all, if not all, truth claims are of this sort, from claiming that there is a tree in the garden (it could be a mirage) to claiming that all water boils at 100° (we can't show that it could never happen that one day a kettle of water will boil at 200°). The only areas where we can get total undoubtable certainty are maths and formal logic, and neither of these applies in the real world. No triangle in the real world has perfectly straight sides and internal angles that add up to exactly two right angles. Logical formulae are only ever hypothetical, and tell us nothing about what actually applies in the real world. So to have truth at all in the real world, we must reject the demand for this kind of mathematical or logical proof.

217

This has significant implications for our attempts to prove the existence of God or the truth of Christianity or any world view. Traditionally, the arguments for God's existence have been rejected because they are not logically watertight; but those who tried to make them logically watertight were as misguided as those who rejected them on those grounds. Proof of the existence of God or the truth of a world view is much more like proof of the existence of quarks, or that the defendant is guilty.

For most people the strongest form of proof is personal experience; even the fact that we sometimes make mistakes over what we are experiencing, or perhaps rather in our interpretation of what we are experiencing, doesn't put us off; we develop ways of spotting and correcting the mistakes and feel all the more confident we've got it right the next time round.

★ ★ ★

God and truth

It is time to develop a point we have already touched on when we were looking at the basis for truth, and when we outlined the ancient Hebrew concept. It is the relationship between God and truth.

There are a number of ways we could picture this. Truth could have nothing to do with God. Truth could be God. Or God could be truth. God could be the source of truth. He could communicate truth. Truth could be something created by God but independent of God. God could be the foundation or the guarantee of truth. God could be in some way subject to truth. Or he could arbitrarily decide what is true and what is not.

Thinkers, including Christian thinkers, have explored all of these possibilities. You'll not be surprised to learn that my answer incorporates several of them. Certainly I would want to say that God is the ultimate source of truth. If he is Creator and upholder of everything, then everything must have him as its ultimate source. I don't see this, however, as meaning that each bit of truth has to be individually created by God and maintained by him. Perhaps there is a parallel with love. God is the source of love in that he has created human (and other) persons with a capacity to reflect and express the love that he himself is constantly pouring out on everything that is; so when I express love I am in a sense expressing the heart and being of God. But it is still me expressing it; God has trusted me with the capacity to express something of himself.

In a similar way he has created us with the ability to know and express truth; it is truth that has its source in him, but I receive it and express it. Truth radiates from him as light chasing away the darkness, but I share in the process of spreading the light.

There is, of course, another, more immediate, sense in which God is the source of truth. If God is personal we might expect him to be involved in personal relationship with personal creatures he has made; a God of love will want to give and experience love in those relationships; a holy God will seek to share his goodness with us; a God of life will enrich our lives with his; and a God of truth will communicate truth to us.

The concept of God communicating truth is central to Christianity, whether it is by revelation, through the Word made flesh, through what the Holy Spirit is saying, or through the Scriptures. Sadly, the debate over the technicalities of revelation has sometimes diverted attention from the central concept, just as debate over Genesis 1 has diverted attention from what it means to have God as Creator. But the heart of the matter is that God communicates, as a person, in our beings, and through words; and all his communication is truth.

In what way could we say truth is God or God is truth? I prefer the second way of putting it, in that it seems to allow that God can be other things besides truth – light and love, for example. To say that God is truth could be taken as meaning that everything that God is or says or does is permeated through and through with truth: there is nothing false about him; he never tells a lie; everything he does is consistent and trustworthy, and so on. This is undoubtedly so; but perhaps there is an even deeper way we could understand the concept that God is truth. We could argue that a woman might have nothing false about her; she never tells lies; all she does is consistent and trustworthy, and so on; but that would not make us say, 'She is truth.' If we say 'God is truth' we are saying all those things plus something extra. The something extra is that besides being full of truth and living truth and telling truth and showing truth he *is* truth. The very being of God is truth. Truth is not something additional that he might or might not have, as it is with us. Truth is the essence of God, as life and love and holiness are; it is something inseparable from him.

Here again we are approaching a point where the concepts of truth and goodness and love, and even life, begin to merge into one another, for they are all expressions of who God is; these four things are not four parts of God; they are closely integrated expressions of his being and nature. Indeed, theologians tell us that when Jesus said, 'I am the way and the truth and the life' he wasn't so much giving himself three titles, or describing three parts of his nature; he was making a single statement about himself that needed three of our concepts to put it across. God is what God is; we may in part understand some things about him, and, for our convenience, categorize the parts we do know into things like love and truth and life. But what we are observing and experiencing is one.

Given that God both is the source of truth and is truth,

it is fairly easy to move on and accept that God is the foundation or guarantee of truth. In chapter six Chris outlined the traditional Christian concept (using rather traditional Christian language) of God as guaranteeing truth. Modern western science was founded on the conviction that we could discover truth about the world around us precisely because the creator is consistent and trustworthy, and has made us in his image, such that we could 'think God's thoughts after him'. The last century has seen the loss of the concept of fixed and dependable truth for no other reason than that God has no place in our thinking. For well over two thousand years he had provided a foundation on which truth could be known and built; once that foundation was removed, truth itself collapsed.

In what ways might we see God as guaranteeing truth today? There is one very basic way: unless there is a Creator God whose design and purpose gives meaning to everything that is, there can be no meaning in the universe; and if there is no meaning there can be no truth.

We have a straight choice between saying that the world is the product of chance and saying that it is created by God. The accepted scientific view of this century has been that everything is the result of chance: no design, no plan, no purpose, no meaning, no God; just random happenings, chance events. But chance meaningless events cannot give rise to meaning; however many random movements a particle may make it will not produce a plan or a purpose. A universe in which everything happens by chance could never produce meaning; and without meaning there can be no truth.

Suppose you stood on the top of a cliff and saw that the receding tide had left the usual collection of seaweed, plastic bottles and bits of wood on the beach. Where each bit had been left was, of course, purely by chance, the result of the random movement of the waves – no plan or design or meaning. Yet from your cliff top, amazingly, the rubbish spells out the message *The treasure is buried on the south side of the well by St Erwain's Chapel.* Would you get your pick and shovel and start digging? Not if you really accepted that the arrangement of the rubbish was purely by chance. You would simply mutter, 'What an amazing freak random occurrence', and continue your walk. If the message is the product of chance it can be neither meaningful nor true. Meaning can't come from non-meaning; truth can't come from chance.

So to have meaning and truth at all we must reject the 'Everything is the result of chance' belief, and replace it with something that puts design and purpose and meaning into everything. It is significant that more and more thinkers are recognizing this, for a variety of reasons, and are putting forward suggestions about what might replace chance as the basis of the universe, like cumulative selection or the anthropic principle. But the only one that does not involve meaning in some way or another arising from non-meaning is God. Truth has to have God as its foundation and guarantee.

★ ★ ★

Whatever happened to truth?

Not a lot. Truth itself remains much as it always has been: rich and good, consistent and comprehensive, rational and practical and personal, woven inseparably into the nature of the universe and human life and God, something bigger and more complex than most of us imagine.

But a lot has happened to our view of truth. The traditional Western view has been largely forgotten. The view of the Age of Reason has been vigorously repudiated. The concept of truth on which modern science has been built has been undermined. The suggestion that we can manage without truth is still being made, but has been found wanting. We can expect to see all sorts of new concepts and ideas being put forward in the next few decades.

*   *   *

And what will happen to truth?

It will continue whether we believe it or not, whether we get our ideas about it right or wrong. It will outlive each philosophy and theory and fashion. It will continue to be the standard by which our concepts and words and lives are judged, whether we accept or refuse its judgment. And it will continue to be open to each of us, so that we can seek it and explore it and be enriched by it and build our lives on it and open up its riches for the good of others and the whole of Planet Earth.

Glossary

Age of Reason The Enlightenment period, in which reason was seen as the key to knowledge and happiness.

anthropic principle A theory that without the intervention of God as Creator the universe has the features it has because it is just these which are needed for human persons to exist.

cumulative case The adding together of a number of separate arguments, none of which is convincing in itself, to provide a convincing overall case.

cumulative selection A theory that rejects the idea of evolution by a huge series of chance steps in favour of a process where later steps or selections learn from and are built on earlier ones.

Enlightenment A philosophical movement largely in the seventeenth and eighteenth centuries which stressed reason as the source and judge of all knowledge and truth, and was particularly critical of tradition, accepted institutions, superstition and non-rational elements in religion.

epistemology The philosophical investigation of the nature of and grounds for knowledge, belief and truth.

fallacy Any false step in a process of reasoning or logic.

foundationalism The view that we can know some truths for certain (for example self-evident truths like $2 + 2 = 4$, 'I exist'), and build up a body of knowledge on these as its foundation.

Freudian aggression Sigmund Freud (1856–1939) held that aggression was a basic and essential drive in all human persons.

objective truth Beliefs whose truth is located outside of the person believing them, usually in the object of belief. The truth remains the same, even if no one actually believes it.

paradigm A comprehensive theory, a framework for understanding.

postmodernism A contemporary reaction to the Enlightenment's stress on reason (which gave rise to modernism). Its hallmarks are irrationalism, relativism, and the rejection of structures.

pragmatism An approach that makes the practical outworking of our beliefs the key to their meaningfulness and truth, e.g. William James's statement: 'If the hypothesis of God works satisfactorily in the widest sense of the word, it is true.'

presuppositions Foundational beliefs which we accept without proof and on which we build our world view.

quarks Hypothetical elementary particles.

rationalism An approach which makes reason the source and judge of knowledge and truth.

realism The belief that the external world is real, that it exists independently of us, and that (however partially and imperfectly) we can know things about it that are true.

relativism A rejection of fixed unchanging timeless truth that we can know. All 'truth' is relative to the person, culture, situation etc. in which it is believed; what is true for me, true today, true in the UK, will not necessarily be true for you, true tomorrow, true in Asia.

scepticism The rejection of knowledge; any 'truth' can be doubted, so nothing can be certain, therefore nothing can be known.

subjective truth Beliefs whose truth is located in the person believing them, the believing subject; if no one holds such a belief it would not be true.

sub-nuclear physics The science of the particles that make up the nucleus of an atom.

syllogism A logical argument of the form:

All men are mortal
Socrates is a man
Therefore Socrates is mortal.

undistributed middle A specific logical error which makes a syllogism invalid, e.g.

A. All oaks are trees
A beech is a tree
Therefore a beech is an oak

B. All trees are oaks
A beech is a tree
Therefore a beech is an oak.

In A the 'middle' term 'trees / tree' is not 'distributed' (it doesn't cover all possible trees), so the syllogism is invalid; in B it is 'distributed' ('all trees') so B is logically valid (though false!).

For further reading

There is a great deal of literature on the subject of knowledge and truth, mostly written by philosophers for philosophers and pretty inaccessible to ordinary people. But there are some more readable books. One of them, a short and reasonably easy introduction, is:
DL Wolfe *Epistemology* IVP 1982.

Lesslie Newbigin is always good to read; truth, belief and knowledge are dealt with in the opening sections of the following:
L Newbigin *The Gospel in a Pluralist Society* SPCK 1991
L Newbigin *Truth to Tell* SPCK 1991.

A key book, although less easy, in which a group of Christian philosophers grapple with the issues, is:
A Plantinga and N Wolterstorff (eds) *Faith and Rationality* Notre Dame 1983.

There are a number of books that are made up of selections of what thinkers through the centuries have written about knowledge and truth. Parts of them will be difficult reading, but sometimes even philosophers manage to write clearly. Two such books are:
PK Moser and A vd Nat *Human Knowledge: Classical and Contemporary Approaches* Oxford University Press 1995.
L Pojman *The Theory of Knowledge* Wadsworth 1993.

Index